David
A Man After God's Own Heart

Ellen G. White

TEACH Services, Inc.
PUBLISHING
www.TEACHServices.com • (800) 367-1844

World rights reserved. This book or any portion thereof may not be copied or reproduced in any form or manner whatever, except as provided by law, without the written permission of the publisher, except by a reviewer who may quote brief passages in a review.

The author assumes full responsibility for the accuracy and interpretation of the Ellen White quotations cited in this book. Unless otherwise indicated, all scripture quotations are taken from the King James Version of the Bible.

The ESV® Bible (The Holy Bible, English Standard Version®). ESV® Text Edition: 2016. Copyright © 2001 by Crossway, a publishing ministry of Good News Publishers. The ESV® text has been reproduced in cooperation with and by permission of Good News Publishers. Unauthorized reproduction of this publication is prohibited. All rights reserved.

THE HOLY BIBLE, NEW INTERNATIONAL VERSION®, NIV® Copyright © 1973, 1978, 1984, 2011 by Biblica, Inc.™ Used by permission. All rights reserved worldwide.

Passages labeled (AMP) are taken from the Amplified Bible. All rights reserved. For Permission To Quote information visit http://www.lockman.org. The "Amplified" trademark is registered in the United States Patent and Trademark Office by The Lockman Foundation. Use of this trademark requires the permission of The Lockman Foundation.

Passages labeled (TLNT) are taken from the Theological Lexicon of the New Testament, ©1995 by Hendrickson Publications.

Passages labeled (WEB) are taken from the World English Bible. Public domain.

Copyright © 2019 TEACH Services, Inc.

ISBN-13: 978-1-4796-1106-5 (Paperback)

ISBN-13: 978-1-4796-1107-2 (ePub)

Library of Congress Control Number: 2019938838

And when he had removed him [Saul], he raised up unto them David to be their king; to whom also he gave testimony, and said, I have found David the son of Jesse, a man after mine own heart, which shall fulfil all my will.

Acts 13:22.

Table of Contents

Chapter One: David's Youth 7
Chapter Two: The Young Man 24
Chapter Three: David In Exile 32
Chapter Four: David Crowned King 66
Chapter Five: David's Moral Fall 81
Chapter Six: Absalom's Rebellion 92
Chapter Seven: The King's Final Years 107
Bibliography 114

Chapter One

David's Youth

A few miles south of Jerusalem, "the city of the great King," is Bethlehem, where David, the son of Jesse, was born more than a thousand years before the infant Jesus was cradled in the manger and worshiped by the Wise Men from the East. Centuries before the advent of the Saviour, David, in the freshness of boyhood, kept watch of his flocks as they grazed on the hills surrounding Bethlehem. The simple shepherd boy sang the songs of his own composing, and the music of his harp made a sweet accompaniment to the melody of his fresh young voice. The Lord had chosen David, and was preparing him, in his solitary life with his flocks, for the work He designed to commit to his trust in after years.

Samuel Anoints David

While David was thus living in the retirement of his humble shepherd's life, the Lord God was speaking about him to the prophet Samuel. "And the Lord said unto Samuel, How long wilt thou mourn for Saul, seeing I have rejected him from reigning over Israel? fill thine horn with oil, and go, I will send thee to Jesse the Bethlehemite: for I have provided Me a king among his sons....

Take an heifer with thee, and say, I am come to sacrifice to the Lord. And call Jesse to the sacrifice, and I will show thee what thou shalt do: and thou shalt anoint unto Me him whom I name unto thee. And Samuel did that which the Lord spake, and came to Bethlehem. And the elders of the town trembled at his coming, and said, Comest thou peaceably? And he said, Peaceably." The elders accepted an invitation to the sacrifice, and Samuel called also Jesse and his sons. The altar was built and the sacrifice was ready. All the household of Jesse were present, with the exception of David, the youngest son, who had been left to guard the sheep, for it was not safe to leave the flocks unprotected. *Patriarchs and Prophets,* 637.

But who is capable of selecting from a family of children the ones upon whom will rest the most important responsibilities? How often human judgment has here proved to be at fault! Remember the experience of Samuel when sent to anoint from the sons of Jesse one to be king over Israel. Seven noble-looking youth passed before him. As he looked upon the first, in features comely, in form well-developed, and in bearing princely, the prophet exclaimed, "Surely the Lord's anointed is before Him." But God said, "Look not on his countenance, or on the height of his stature; because I have refused him: for the Lord seeth not as man seeth; for man looketh on the outward appearance, but the Lord looketh on the heart." So of all the seven the testimony was, "The Lord hath not chosen these." 1 Samuel 16:6, 7, 10. And not until David had been called from the flock was the prophet permitted to fulfill his mission.

> *So today, in many a child whom the parents would pass by, God sees capabilities far above those revealed by others who are thought to possess great promise*

The elder brothers, from whom Samuel would have chosen, did not possess the qualifications that God saw to be essential in a ruler of His people. Proud, self-centered, self-confident, they were set aside for the one whom they lightly regarded, one who had preserved the simplicity and sincerity of his youth, and who, while little in his own sight, could be trained by God for the responsibilities of the kingdom. So today, in many a child whom the parents would pass by, God sees capabilities far above those revealed by others who are thought to possess great promise. *Education*, 266.

The lonely shepherd was startled by the unexpected call of the messenger, who announced that the prophet had come to Bethlehem and had sent for him. With surprise he questioned why the prophet and judge of Israel should desire to see him; but without delay he obeyed the call. "Now he was ruddy, and withal of a beautiful countenance, and goodly to look to." As Samuel beheld with pleasure the handsome, manly, modest shepherd boy, the voice of the Lord spoke to the prophet, saying, "Arise, anoint him: for this is he." David had proved himself brave and faithful in the humble office of a shepherd, and now God had chosen him to be captain of His people. "Then Samuel took the horn of oil, and anointed him in the midst of [from among] his brethren: and the Spirit of the Lord came upon David from that day forward." The prophet had accomplished his appointed work, and with a relieved heart he returned to Ramah.

Samuel had not made known his errand, even to the family of Jesse, and the ceremony of anointing David had been performed in secret. It was an intimation to the youth of the high destiny awaiting him, that amid all the varied experiences and perils of his coming years, this knowledge might inspire him to be true to the purpose of God to be accomplished by his life.

David's Humility

The great honor conferred upon David did not serve to elate him. Notwithstanding the high position which he was to occupy, he quietly continued his employment, content to await the development of the Lord's plans in His own time and way. As humble and modest as before his anointing, the shepherd boy returned to the hills and watched and guarded his flocks as tenderly as ever. But with new inspiration he composed his melodies and played upon his harp. Before him spread a landscape of rich and varied beauty. The vines, with their clustering fruit, brightened in the sunshine. The forest trees, with their green foliage, swayed in the breeze. He beheld the sun flooding the heavens with light, coming forth as a bridegroom out of his chamber and rejoicing as a strong man to run a race. There were the bold summits of the hills reaching toward the sky; in the faraway distance rose the barren cliffs of the mountain wall of Moab; above all spread the tender blue of the overarching heavens. And beyond was God. He could not see Him, but His works were full of His praise. The light of day, gilding forest and mountain, meadow and stream, carried the mind up to behold the Father of lights, the Author of every good and perfect gift. Daily revelations of the character and majesty of his Creator filled the young poet's heart with adoration and rejoicing. In contemplation of God and His works the faculties of David's mind and heart were developing and strengthening for the work of his afterlife. He was daily coming into a more intimate communion with God. His mind was constantly penetrating into new depths for fresh themes to inspire his song and to wake the music of his harp. The rich melody of his voice poured out upon the air, echoed from the hills as if responsive to the rejoicing of the angels' songs in heaven.

Who can measure the results of those years of toil and wandering among the lonely hills? The communion with nature and with God, the care of his flocks, the perils and deliverances, the griefs and joys, of his lowly lot, were not only to mold the character of David and to influence his future life, but through the psalms of Israel's sweet singer they were in all coming ages to kindle love and faith in the hearts of God's people, bringing them nearer to the ever-loving heart of Him in whom all His creatures live.

David, in the beauty and vigor of his young manhood, was preparing to take a high position with the noblest of the earth. His talents, as precious gifts from God, were employed to extol the glory of the divine Giver. His opportunities of contemplation and meditation served to enrich him with that wisdom and piety that made him beloved of God and angels. As he contemplated the perfections of his Creator, clearer conceptions of God opened before his soul. Obscure themes were illuminated, difficulties were made plain, perplexities were harmonized, and each ray of new light called forth fresh bursts of rapture, and sweeter anthems of devotion, to the glory of God and the Redeemer. The love that moved him, the sorrows that beset him, the triumphs that attended him, were all themes for his active thought; and as he beheld the love of God in all the providences of his life, his heart throbbed with more fervent adoration and gratitude, his voice rang out in a richer melody, his harp was swept with more exultant joy; and the shepherd boy proceeded from strength to strength, from knowledge to knowledge; for the Spirit of the Lord was upon him. *Patriarchs and Prophets,* 641, 642.

The principles taught in the schools of the prophets were the same that molded David's character and shaped his life. The word of God was his instructor. "Through Thy precepts," he said, "I get understanding. I have inclined mine heart to perform Thy statutes." Psalm 119:104–112. It was this that caused the Lord to pronounce David, when in his youth He called him to the throne, "a man after Mine own heart." Acts 13:22. *Education,* 48.

David's Talents Recommended to Saul

When Saul saw that Samuel came no more to instruct him, he knew that the Lord had rejected him for his wicked course, and his character seemed ever after to be marked with extremes. ... He was melancholy, and often afraid when there was no danger. This disqualified him for being ruler. He was always full of anxiety;

and when in his gloomy moods, he wished not to be disturbed, and at times would suffer none to approach him. He would speak prophetically of his being dethroned, and another's occupying his position as ruler, and that his posterity would never be exalted to the throne, and receive kingly honors, but that they would all perish because of his sins. He would repeat, prophetically, sayings against himself with distracted energy, even in the presence of his lords, and of the people.

Those who witnessed these strange exhibitions in Saul recommended to him music, as calculated to have a soothing influence upon his mind when thus distracted. In the providence of God, David was brought to his notice as a skillful musician. He was also recommended for being a valiant man of war, prudent and faithful in all matters, because he was especially guided by the Lord. Saul felt humbled at times, and was even anxious that one should take charge of the government of the kingdom, who should know from the Lord how to move in accordance with his will. While in a favorable state of mind, he sent messengers for David. He soon loved him, and gave him the position of armor-bearer, making him his attendant. He thought that if David was favored of God, he would be a safeguard to him, and perhaps save his life, when he should be exposed to his enemies. David's skillful playing upon the harp soothed the troubled spirit of Saul. As he listened to the enchanting strains of music, it had an influence to dispel the gloom which had settled upon him, and to bring his excited mind into a more rational, happy state. *Spirit of Prophecy*, vol. 1, 368.

In the providence of God, David, as a skillful performer upon the harp, was brought before the king. The shepherd boy was employed to play before the ruler of Israel, and, if possible, to charm away the brooding melancholy which had settled, like a dark cloud, over the mind of Saul. The king was ever occupied in anticipating the ruin that had been brought upon his house by his own course of disobedience and rebellion. It was not true repentance that had bowed the proud head of Saul. He had no perception of the offensive character of his sin in the sight of God, and he did not arouse to reform his life and character. His heart was not humbled because he had disregarded the express injunctions and commands of the Ruler of the universe; therefore he did not return to his allegiance to the Head of all kingdoms, but brooded over what he thought was the injustice of God in depriving him of the throne of Israel, and in taking the succession to its privileges away from his posterity. He felt that the valor which he had displayed in encountering his enemies, should offset his sin of disobedience. He did not accept with meekness the chastisement of God; but his proud spirit became desperate, until he was on the verge of losing his reason.

David came before Saul, and played with all the skill that his long practice had given him; and his lofty and Heaven-inspired strains had the desired effect. The evil spirit seemed to be driven away, and the king was restored to his usual calmness. As David stood, for the first time, in the presence of Saul, there were many thoughts that filled the mind of the young musician, and served to fasten this scene upon his memory with an indelible impression. When his services were not required at the court of Saul, David returned to his flocks on the hills, and continued to maintain his simplicity of spirit and demeanor. Whenever it was necessary, he was recalled to minister before the king, to soothe the mind of the troubled monarch till the evil spirit departed from him. But although Saul expressed the greatest delight in David and

David was growing in favor with God and man. He had been instructed in the way of the Lord, and he now set his heart more fully to do the will of God than ever before

his music, the young shepherd went from the king's house to the fields and hills of his pasture, with a sense of relief and gladness, to care for his flocks with a tender and faithful care. *Signs of the Times*, August 3, 1888.

David in his youth was intimately associated with Saul, and his stay at court and his connection with the king's household gave him an insight into the cares and sorrows and perplexities concealed by the glitter and pomp of royalty. He saw of how little worth is human glory to bring peace to the soul. And it was with relief and gladness that he returned from the king's court to the sheepfolds and the flocks. *Education*, 152.

David was growing in favor with God and man. He had been instructed in the way of the Lord, and he now set his heart more fully to do the will of God than ever before. He had new themes for thought. He had been in the court of the king and had seen the responsibilities of royalty. He had discovered some of the temptations that beset the soul of Saul and had penetrated some of the mysteries in the character and dealings of Israel's first king. He had seen the glory of royalty shadowed with a dark cloud of sorrow, and he knew that the household of Saul, in their private life, were far from happy. All these things served to bring troubled thoughts to him who had been anointed to be king over Israel. But while he was absorbed in deep meditation, and harassed by thoughts of anxiety, he turned to his harp, and called forth strains that elevated his mind to the Author of every good, and the dark clouds that seemed to shadow the horizon of the future were dispelled.

God was teaching David lessons of trust. As Moses was trained for his work, so the Lord was fitting the son of Jesse to become the guide of His chosen people. In his watchcare for his flocks, he was gaining an appreciation of the care that the Great Shepherd has for the sheep of His pasture. *Patriarchs and Prophets*, 643, 644.

Courage in Youth

The lonely hills and the wild ravines where David wandered with his flocks were the lurking place of beasts of prey. Not infrequently the lion from the thickets by the Jordan, or the bear from his lair among the hills, came, fierce with hunger, to attack the flocks. According to the custom of his time, David was armed only with his sling and shepherd's staff; yet he early gave proof of his strength and courage in protecting his charge. Afterward describing these encounters, he said: "When there came a lion, or a bear, and took a lamb out of the flock, I went out after him, and smote him, and delivered it out of his mouth: and when he arose against me, I caught him by his beard, and smote him, and slew him." 1 Samuel 17:34, 35, R.V. His experience in these matters proved the heart of David and developed in him courage and fortitude and faith. *Patriarchs and Prophets*, 644.

On one occasion, as the evening shadows gathered, and he laid aside his harp, he saw a dark form moving stealthily upon his flock. It was a bear, fierce with hunger, that sprang upon the sheep of his care; but David did not flee for his life. He felt that it was the very hour when his charges needed his protection. He lifted his heart to God in prayer for wisdom and help, that he might do his duty in this time of peril. With his strong arm he laid the bear in death at his feet. At another time he discovered a lion with a bleeding lamb between his jaws. Without hesitation the youthful shepherd engaged in a desperate encounter. His arm, nerved by the living God, forced the beast to release its bleeding victim, and as it turned, mad with disappointment, upon David, he buried his hand in its mane and killed the fierce invader. His experience in these matters proved the heart of David, and developed in him courage, and fortitude, and faith. God was teaching David lessons of trust. As Moses was trained for his work, so the Lord was fitting the son of Jesse to become the leader and guide of his chosen people. In his watch-care for his flocks, he was gaining an appreciation of the care that the great Shepherd has for the sheep of his pasture. *Signs of the Times*, August 3, 1888.

David and Goliath

Even before he was summoned to the court of Saul, David had distinguished himself by deeds of valor. The officer who brought him to the notice of the king declared him to be "a mighty valiant man, and a man of war, and prudent in matters," and he said, "The Lord is with him."

When war was declared by Israel against the Philistines, three of the sons of Jesse joined the army under Saul; but David remained at home. After a time, however, he went to visit the camp of Saul. By his father's direction he was to carry a message and a gift to his elder brothers and to learn if they were still in safety and health. But, unknown to Jesse, the youthful shepherd had been entrusted with a higher mission. The armies of Israel were in peril, and David had been directed by an angel to save his people.

As David drew near to the army, he heard the sound of commotion, as if an engagement was about to begin. And "the host was going forth to the fight, and shouted for the battle." Israel and the Philistines were drawn up in array, army against army. David ran to the army, and came and saluted his brothers. While he was talking with them, Goliath, the champion of the Philistines, came forth, and with insulting language defied Israel and challenged them to provide a man from their ranks who would meet him in single combat. He repeated his challenge, and when David saw that all Israel were filled with fear, and learned that the Philistine's defiance was hurled at them day after day, without arousing a champion to silence the boaster, his spirit was stirred within him. He was fired with zeal to preserve the honor of the living God and the credit of His people.

The armies of Israel were depressed. Their courage failed. They said one to another, "Have ye seen this man that is come up? surely to defy Israel is he come up." In shame and indignation, David exclaimed, "Who is this uncircumcised Philistine, that he should defy the armies of the living God?"

Eliab, David's eldest brother, when he heard these words, knew well the feelings that were stirring the young man's soul. Even as a shepherd, David had manifested daring, courage, and strength but rarely witnessed; and the mysterious visit of Samuel to their father's house, and his silent departure, had awakened in the minds of the brothers suspicions of the real object of his visit. Their jealousy had been aroused as they saw David honored above them, and they did not regard him with the respect and love due to his integrity and brotherly tenderness. They looked upon him as merely a stripling shepherd, and now the question which he asked was regarded by Eliab as a censure upon his own cowardice in making no attempt to silence the giant of the Philistines. The elder brother exclaimed angrily, "Why camest thou down hither? and with whom hast thou left those few sheep in the wilderness? I know thy pride, and the naughtiness of thine heart; for thou art come down that thou mightest see the battle." David's answer was respectful but decided: "What have I now done? Is there not a cause?" *Patriarchs and Prophets*, 644, 645.

David is not careful to explain to his brother that he had come to the help of Israel; that God had sent him to slay Goliath. God had chosen him to be a ruler of Israel; and as the armies of the living God were in such peril, he had been directed by an angel to save Israel. *Spirit of Prophecy*, vol. 1, 371.

David was visiting his brothers in the camp of Saul; he heard this proud boaster defying Israel, and his spirit was stirred within him. He was jealous for the armies of the living God, and indignant that a heathen, who had no fear of God, and no power from him, should thus hold all Israel in fear, and triumph over them. He did not boast of his own superior skill; but surely in the strength of God he could overcome this mighty warrior. *Our Australian Youth*, March 1, 1888.

The words of David were repeated to the king, who summoned the youth before him. Saul listened with astonishment to the words of the shepherd, as he said, "Let no man's heart fail because of him; thy servant will go and fight with this Philistine." Saul strove to turn David from his purpose, but the young man was not to be moved. He replied in a simple, unassuming way, relating his experiences while guarding his father's flocks. And he said, "The Lord that delivered me out of the paw of the lion, and out of the paw of the bear, He will deliver me out of the hand of this Philistine. And Saul said unto David, Go, and the Lord be with thee." *Patriarchs and Prophets*, 646.

Modest and Unassuming

Was it presumption that led David to think that he might be a match for Goliath? Was it a spirit of pride and self-sufficiency that made him dare to meet this mighty warrior who was defying the Israel of God? David had none of this spirit. Modest and unassuming, he did not make this declaration trusting in his own wisdom, skill, or power, but in the strength of God, who had delivered him out of the paw of the lion and the bear when he was watching his father's flocks in the wilderness. *Signs of the Times*, March 4, 1886.

Though Saul had given David permission to accept Goliath's challenge, the king had small hope that David would be successful in his courageous undertaking. Command was given to clothe the youth in the king's own armor. The heavy helmet of brass was put upon his head, and the coat of mail was placed upon his body; the monarch's sword was at his side. Thus equipped, he started upon his errand, but erelong began to retrace his steps. The first thought in the minds of the anxious spectators was that David had decided not to risk his life in meeting an antagonist in so unequal an encounter. But this was far from the thought of the brave young man. When he returned to Saul he begged permission to lay aside the heavy armor, saying, "I cannot go with these; for I have not proved them." He laid off the king's armor, and in its stead took only his staff in his hand, with his shepherd's scrip and a simple sling. Choosing five smooth stones out of the brook, he put them in his bag, and, with his sling in his hand, drew near to the Philistine. The giant strode boldly forward, expecting to meet the mightiest of the warriors of Israel. His armor-bearer walked before him, and he looked as if nothing could withstand him. As he came nearer to David he saw but a stripling, called a boy because of his youth. David's countenance was ruddy with health, and his well-knit form, unprotected by armor, was displayed to advantage; yet between its youthful outline and the massive proportions of the Philistine, there was a marked contrast.

David Stands Bravely

Goliath was filled with amazement and anger. "Am I a dog," he exclaimed, "that thou comest to me with staves?" Then he poured upon David the most terrible curses by all the gods of his knowledge. He cried in derision, "Come to me, and I will give thy flesh unto the fowls of the air, and to the beasts of the field."

David did not weaken before the champion of the Philistines. Stepping forward, he said to his antagonist: "Thou comest to me with a sword, and with a spear, and with a shield: but I come to thee in the name of the Lord of hosts, the God of the armies of Israel, whom thou hast defied. This day will the Lord deliver thee into mine hand; and I will smite thee, and take thine head from thee; and I will give the carcasses of the host of the Philistines this day unto the fowls of the air, and to the wild beasts of the earth; that all the earth may know that there is a God in Israel. And all this assembly shall know that the Lord saveth not with sword and spear: for the battle is the Lord's, and He will give you into our hands."

There was a ring of fearlessness in his tone, a look of triumph and rejoicing upon his fair countenance. This speech, given in a clear, musical voice, rang out on the air, and was distinctly heard by the listening thousands marshaled for war. The anger of Goliath was roused to the very highest heat. In his rage he pushed up the helmet that protected his forehead and rushed forward to wreak vengeance upon his opponent. *Patriarchs and Prophets*, 646–648.

With what anxious interest do both armies watch the unequal combat. The Philistines and many of the Israelites think David foolhardy; but this is but for a moment. As he runs to meet Goliath, he adjusts a stone in the sling, and presently it has sped to its mark, and is imbedded in the forehead of the giant. A dimness comes over his sight; he reels, and falls heavily to the ground, like some mighty oak overthrown by a lightning stroke. Consternation seizes upon the Philistines, and they make a confused and hasty retreat. The warriors of Israel, with a shout of triumph, follow the flying hosts, and the victory is complete.

> *Here we have an example of lofty courage, of a humble, but living faith. David's trust was not in himself*

Here we have an example of lofty courage, of a humble, but living faith. David's trust was not in himself, neither was his motive a selfish one. But he was ready, in the strength of God, to meet Israel's foe, to test Jehovah's might against a heathen giant, that he might "take away the reproach from Israel." This was the divine plan for distinguishing David, Israel's future king, and for humbling the adversaries of the true God. *Signs of the Times*, March 4, 1886.

David's Modesty in Saul's Court

After the slaying of Goliath David was brought before King Saul, and the king inquired concerning his parentage and life. "And it came to pass, when he had made an end of speaking unto Saul, that the soul of Jonathan was knit with the soul of David, and Jonathan loved him as his own soul." Saul kept David with him, and would not permit him to return to his father's house. Jonathan and David made a covenant to be united as brethren, and the king's son "stripped himself of the robe that was upon him, and gave it to David, and his garments, even to his sword, and to his bow, and to his girdle." David was intrusted with important responsibilities, yet he preserved his modesty, and everyone loved him. But there was no one so dear to him as Jonathan, because he possessed a pure and noble spirit. *Signs of the Times*, August 17, 1888.

"David went out whithersoever Saul sent him, and behaved himself wisely: and Saul set him over the men of war." David was prudent and faithful, and it was evident that the blessing of God was with him. Saul at times realized his own unfitness for the government of Israel, and he felt that the kingdom would be more secure if there could be connected with him one who received instruction from the Lord. Saul hoped also that his connection with David would be a safeguard to himself. Since David was favored and shielded by the Lord, his presence might be a protection to Saul when he went out with him to war.

It was the providence of God that had connected David with Saul. David's position at court would give him a knowledge of affairs, in preparation for his future greatness. It would enable him to gain the confidence of the nation. The vicissitudes and hardships which befell him, through the enmity of Saul, would lead him to feel his dependence upon God, and to put his whole trust in Him. And the friendship of Jonathan for David was also of God's providence, to preserve the life of the future ruler of Israel. In all these things God was working out His gracious purposes, both for David and for the people of Israel. *Patriarchs and Prophets*, 649.

David Endures Saul's Jealousy

"David went out whithersoever Saul sent him, and behaved himself wisely. And Saul set him over the men of war." But when Saul and David were returning from the slaughter of the Philistines, "the women came out of all cities of Israel, singing and dancing, to meet King Saul, with tabrets, with joy, and with instruments of music." One company sang, "Saul hath slain his thousands," while another company took up the strain and responded, "And David his ten thousands." The demon of jealousy entered the heart of the king. He was angry because David was exalted above himself in the song of the women of Israel. In place of controlling these envious feelings, and manifesting a noble spirit, he displayed the great weakness of his character, and exclaimed, "They have ascribed unto David ten thousands, and to me they have ascribed but thousands; and what can he have more but the kingdom?" *Signs of the Times*, August 17, 1888.

Saul opened his heart to the spirit of jealousy by which his soul was poisoned. Notwithstanding the lessons which he had received from the prophet Samuel, instructing him that God would accomplish whatsoever He chose, and that no one could hinder it, the king made it evident that he had no true knowledge of the plans or power of God. The monarch of Israel was opposing his will to the will of the Infinite One. Saul had not learned, while ruling the kingdom of Israel, that he should rule his own spirit. He allowed his impulses to control his judgment, until he was plunged into a fury of passion. He had paroxysms of rage, when he was ready to take the life of any who dared oppose his will. From this frenzy he would pass into a state of despondency and self-contempt, and remorse would take possession of his soul.

He loved to hear David play upon his harp, and the evil spirit seemed to be charmed away for the time; but one day when the youth was ministering before him, and bringing sweet music from his instrument, accompanying his voice as he sang the praises of God, Saul suddenly threw his spear at the musician, for the purpose of putting an end to his life. David was preserved by the interposition of God, and without injury fled from the rage of the maddened king. *Patriarchs and Prophets*, 650.

Chapter Two

The Young Man

Through the influence of the people, David was promoted to take charge of the business connected with warfare. He was leader in all their important enterprises. As Saul saw that David had won the love and confidence of the people, he hated him; for he thought that he was preferred before him. He watched an opportunity to slay him; and when the evil spirit was upon him, and David played before him as usual to soothe his troubled mind, he tried to kill him, by throwing with force a sharp-pointed instrument at his heart. Angels of God preserved the life of David. They made him understand what was the purpose of Saul; and as the instrument was hurled at him, he sprang to one side, and received no harm, while the instrument was driven deep into the wall where David had been sitting. *Spirit of Prophecy*, vol. 1, 373.

As Saul's hatred of David increased, he became more and more watchful to find an opportunity to take his life; but none of his plans against the anointed of the Lord were successful. Saul gave himself up to the control of the wicked spirit that ruled over him; while David trusted in Him who is mighty in counsel, and strong to deliver. "The fear of the Lord is the beginning of wisdom" (Proverbs 9:10), and David's prayer was continually directed to God, that he might walk before Him in a perfect way. *Patriarchs and Prophets*, 651.

Especially was the heart of Jonathan knit with David's; and there was a most sacred bond of union established between them, which remained unbroken till the death of Saul and Jonathan. This was the Lord's doings, that Jonathan might be the means of preserving the life of David when Saul would try to kill him. God's providence connected David with Saul, that by his wise behaviour he might obtain the confidence of the people, and by a long course of hardships and vicissitudes, be led to put his entire trust in God, while he was preparing him to become ruler of his people. *Spiritual Gifts,* vol. 4a (1864), 79.

David's Patience with Saul

Saul made David feel that there was no place of security for him. He finally removed him from his position of responsibility as leader of the army of Israel, and placed him in charge of only a thousand men. David made no complaint, but bore all with patience. The love of the people was with him, but Saul was determined that he should not live. He kept a strict watch upon David, longing and hoping to find some occasion of indiscretion or rashness which might serve as an excuse to bring him into disgrace before the people. He felt that he could not be satisfied until he could take the young man's life, and still be justified before the nation for his evil act.

Saul laid a snare for the feet of David, promising to give him Michal, his daughter, to wife, if he would slay one hundred Philistines. David killed two hundred, and returned in safety to the court of the king. Saul was still more assured that this was the man whom the Lord had said was better than he, and who should reign on the throne of Israel in his place. He began to discover that the Lord was with David. He began to discern that the young man was walking circumspectly before God, and that his character was worthy of respect, being truly noble and elevated. Saul became more determined in his purpose. He threw off all disguise. He would not be disappointed. David must die. He issued a command to Jonathan and to his servants to take the life of the one he hated; for he had determined that he should not live.

Jonathan revealed his father's intention to David, and bade him conceal himself, while he would go and plead with his father to spare the life of the deliverer of Israel. Jonathan succeeded in turning away the wrath of his father for the time. He presented before the king what David had done to preserve the honor and the very life of the nation, and what terrible guilt would come upon his soul who should slay the one whom God had used to scatter their enemies. He urged that his crime would not be excused should he take the life of an innocent man. The conscience of the king was touched, and his heart was softened. "And Saul sware, As the Lord liveth, he shall not be slain." And David was brought to Saul, and he ministered in his presence, as he had in the past. *Signs of the Times*, August 17, 1888.

Though Saul was ever on the alert for an opportunity to destroy David, he stood in fear of him, since it was evident that the Lord was with him. David's blameless character aroused the wrath of the king; he deemed that the very life and presence of David cast a reproach upon him, since by contrast it presented his own character to disadvantage. It was envy that made Saul miserable and put the humble subject of his throne in jeopardy. What untold mischief has this evil trait of character worked in our world! The same enmity existed in the heart of Saul that stirred the heart of Cain against his brother Abel, because Abel's works were righteous, and God honored him,

> *Envy is the offspring of pride, and if it is entertained in the heart, it will lead to hatred, and eventually to revenge and murder*

and his own works were evil, and the Lord could not bless him. Envy is the offspring of pride, and if it is entertained in the heart, it will lead to hatred, and eventually to revenge and murder. Satan displayed his own character in exciting the fury of Saul against him who had never done him harm.

The king kept a strict watch upon David, hoping to find some occasion of indiscretion or rashness that might serve as an excuse to bring him into disgrace. He felt that he could not be satisfied until he could take the young man's life and still be justified before the nation for his evil act. He laid a snare for the feet of David, urging him to conduct the war against the Philistines with still greater vigor, and promising, as a reward of his valor, an alliance with the eldest daughter of the royal house. To this proposal David's modest answer was, "Who am I? and what is my life, or my father's family in Israel, that I should be son-in-law to the king?" The monarch manifested his insincerity by wedding the princess to another. *Patriarchs and Prophets*, 651.

After Jonathan had pleaded successfully for the life of his friend, Saul's wrath against David seemed to be allayed. The young man went in before the king as formerly, and was in the favor of Saul and his court. But again war was declared between the Israelites and the Philistines, and David led the army against their enemies. Under his wise management, a great victory was gained by the Hebrews, and the people of the realm praised his valor, and wisdom, and heroism. This served to stir up the former bitterness and hatred of Saul against him. While the young man was playing before the king, filling the palace with sweet harmony, Saul's passion overcame him, and he hurled a javelin at David, thinking to pin the musician to the wall; but the angel of the Lord turned aside the deadly weapon. David escaped, and fled to his own house. Saul sent spies that they might take him as he should come out in the morning, and put an end to his life.

Michal, the daughter of Saul, was David's wife, and she loved him, and informed him of the purpose of her father. She urged him to escape for his life, and let him down from the window, and David fled to Samuel at Naioth. The king sent his men to the chamber of David, but they found nothing but an effigy which his wife had placed in the bed. The king was very angry with his daughter, and, enraged with disappointment, he determined that his hated subject should not escape. The same spirit which had actuated Satan, filled the heart of Saul. Like the first great apostate, he was moved by unholy ambition and murderous rage. And this was the first chosen king of Israel! Since the day when the holy anointing oil had been poured upon his head by the prophet of God, how terrible had been his fall! *Signs of the Times*, August 24, 1888.

David Learns from Samuel

He fled to Samuel at Ramah, and the prophet, fearless of the king's displeasure, welcomed the fugitive. The home of Samuel was a peaceful place in contrast with the royal palace. It was here, amid the hills, that the honored servant of the Lord continued his work. A company of seers was with him, and they studied closely the will of God and listened reverently to the words of instruction that fell from the lips of Samuel. Precious were the lessons that David learned from the teacher of Israel. David believed that the troops of Saul would not be ordered to invade this sacred place, but no place seemed to be sacred to the darkened mind of the desperate king. David's connection with Samuel aroused the jealousy of the king, lest he who was revered as a prophet of God throughout all Israel should lend his influence to the advancement of Saul's rival. When the king learned where David was, he sent officers to bring him to Gibeah, where he intended to carry out his murderous design. *Patriarchs and Prophets*, 653.

But an angel of God met him on the way and controlled him. The Spirit of God held him in Its power, and he went forward uttering prayers to God, interspersed with predictions and sacred melodies. He prophesied of the coming Messiah as the world's

Redeemer. When he came to the prophet's home in Ramah, he laid aside the outer garments that betokened his rank, and all day and all night he lay before Samuel and his pupils, under the influence of the divine Spirit. The people were drawn together to witness this strange scene, and the experience of the king was reported far and wide. Thus again, near the close of his reign, it became a proverb in Israel that Saul also was among the prophets. *Patriarchs and Prophets*, 654.

After the remarkable exhibition of the power of God, Jonathan could not believe that his father would still harm David, for that would be manifest rebellion against God. But notwithstanding the oft-repeated and confident assurances of his friend, David was not convinced. He declared that Saul knew of their attachment for each other, and that this would be a sufficient reason why the king would not make his purposes known to his son. With intense earnestness he rehearsed how he had been driven from place to place, and now he assured Jonathan, "As the Lord liveth, and as thy soul liveth, there is but a step between me and death." *Signs of the Times*, August 24, 1888.

At the time of the new moon a sacred festival was celebrated in Israel. This festival recurred upon the day following the interview between David and Jonathan. At this feast it was expected that both the young men would appear at the king's table; but David feared to be present, and it was arranged that he should visit his brothers in Bethlehem. On his return he was to hide himself in a field not far from the banqueting hall, for three days absenting himself from the presence of the king; and Jonathan would note the effect upon Saul. If inquiry should be made as to the whereabouts of the son of Jesse, Jonathan was to say that he had gone home to attend the sacrifice offered by his father's household. If no angry demonstrations were made by the king, but he should answer, "It is well," then it would be safe for David to return to the court. But if he should become enraged at his absence, it would decide the matter of David's flight.

On the first day of the feast the king made no inquiry concerning the absence of David; but when his place was vacant the second day, he questioned, "Wherefore cometh not the son of Jesse to meat, neither yesterday nor today? And Jonathan answered Saul, David earnestly asked leave of me to go to Bethlehem: and he said, Let me go, I pray thee; for our family hath a sacrifice in the city; and my brother, he hath commanded me to be there: and now, if I have found favor in thine eyes, let me get away, I pray thee, and see my brethren. Therefore he cometh not unto the king's table." When Saul heard these words, his anger was ungovernable. He declared that as long as David lived, Jonathan could not come to the throne of Israel, and he demanded that David should be sent for immediately, that he might be put to death. Jonathan again made intercession for his friend, pleading, "Wherefore shall he be slain? what hath he done?" This appeal to the king only made him more satanic in his fury, and the spear which he had intended for David he now hurled at his own son.

> *"Go in peace, forasmuch as we have sworn both of us in the name of the Lord, saying, The Lord be between me and thee, and between my seed and thy seed forever."*

The prince was grieved and indignant, and leaving the royal presence, he was no more a guest at the feast. His soul was bowed down with sorrow as he repaired at the appointed time to the spot where David was to learn the king's intentions toward him. Each fell upon the other's neck, and they wept bitterly. The dark passion of the king cast its shadow upon the life of the young men, and their grief was too intense for expression. Jonathan's last words fell upon the ear of David as they separated to pursue their different paths, "Go in peace, forasmuch as we have sworn both of us in the name of the Lord, saying, The Lord be between me and thee, and between my seed and thy seed forever." *Patriarchs and Prophets*, 654, 655.

Chapter Three

David in Exile

Jonathan watched the form of his friend until he was lost from sight, lest he should be observed by spies, and taken to the presence of his enemy. Then the king's son returned to Gibeah, and David hastened to reach Nob, a city some ten miles distant, belonging to the tribe of Benjamin. The tabernacle had been taken to this place from Shiloh, and here Ahimelech, the high priest, ministered. David knew not where to fly for refuge, except to the servant of God. The high priest looked upon him with astonishment, as he came unattended, with a countenance marked by anxiety, care, and sorrow. He inquired what had brought him to the place without an attendant. The young man was in constant fear of discovery, and was perplexed as to how he should reply. In his extremity he resorted to deception. Here David manifested a want of faith in God, and his sin resulted in causing the high priest to be put to death. Had the facts been plainly stated, Ahimelech would have known what course to pursue to preserve his life. God requires that truthfulness shall mark his people, even in times of peril. David told the priest that he had been sent by the king to accomplish some secret business which required that he should go alone. He asked the priest for five loaves of bread. There was nothing but hallowed bread in the possession of the man of God; David succeeded, however, in removing his scruples, and obtained the bread to satisfy his hunger.

But a new difficulty now presented itself, which caused fresh anxiety to David. He saw Doeg, the chief of Saul's herdsmen, who had professed the faith of the Hebrews, and who was now paying his vows in the place of worship. The sight of this man decided David to make haste to secure another place of refuge, and to obtain some weapon with which to defend himself if it should become necessary. He knew that Doeg was acquainted with the purpose of Saul in regard to himself. He was aware that orders had been issued to the king's servants to take the life of David if they should find him, and he feared that this man might attempt it before he could make good his escape.

He asked Ahimelech for a sword, and was told that he had none except the sword of Goliath, which had been kept as a relic in the tabernacle. David replied, "There is none like that; give it me." His courage revived as he grasped the sword that he had once used so valiantly to destroy the champion of the Philistines. David fled to Achish, the king of Gath, for he felt that there was more safety in the midst of the enemies of his people than with his own brethren. He decided to throw himself upon the mercies of national foes, rather than stay in the dominions of Saul. *Signs of the Times*, August 31, 1888.

David's First Mistakes

But it was reported to Achish that David was the man who had slain the Philistine champion years before; and now he who had sought refuge with the foes of Israel found himself in great peril. But, feigning madness, he deceived his enemies and thus made his escape.

The first error of David was his distrust of God at Nob, and his second mistake was his deception before Achish. David had displayed noble traits of character, and his moral worth had won him favor with the people; but as trial came upon him, his faith was shaken, and human weakness appeared. He saw in every man a spy and a betrayer. In a great emergency David had looked up to God with a steady eye of faith, and had vanquished the Philistine giant. He believed in God, he went in His name. But as he had been hunted and persecuted, perplexity and distress had nearly hidden his heavenly Father from his sight.

Yet this experience was serving to teach David wisdom; for it led him to realize his weakness and the necessity of constant dependence upon God. Oh, how precious is the sweet influence of the Spirit of God as it comes to depressed or despairing souls, encouraging the fainthearted, strengthening the feeble, and imparting courage and help to the tried servants of the Lord! Oh, what a God is ours, who deals gently with the erring and manifests His patience and tenderness in adversity, and when we are overwhelmed with some great sorrow! *Patriarchs and Prophets*, 656, 657.

> **When shadows encompass the soul, when we want light and guidance, we must look up; there is light beyond the darkness**

While in these trying scenes, he composed some of the psalms. *Signs of the Times*, August 31, 1888.

Every failure on the part of the children of God is due to their lack of faith. When shadows encompass the soul, when we want light and guidance, we must look up; there is light beyond the darkness. David ought not to have distrusted God for one moment. He had cause for trusting in Him: he was the Lord's anointed, and in the midst of danger he had been protected by the angels of God; he had been armed with courage to do wonderful things; and if he had but removed his mind from the distressing situation in which he was placed, and had thought of God's power and majesty, he would have been at peace even in the midst of the shadows of death; he could with confidence have repeated the promise of the Lord, "The mountains shall depart, and the hills be removed; but My kindness shall not depart from thee, neither shall the covenant of My peace be removed." Isaiah 54:10. *Patriarchs and Prophets*, 657.

We see the weakness of even noble men when they are brought into trying circumstances. This man, when in a great emergency, had looked up to God with the steady eye of faith, and had met the proud, boasting Philistine. He believed in God, he went in his name. He trusted in his power to do the work of defeating the armies of the Lord's enemies. But as he had been hunted and persecuted, perplexity and distress had nearly hidden his heavenly Father from his sight. He seemed to think that he was left alone, to fight his own battles. He was confused, and knew not which way to turn. We may learn a lesson from the experience of David. "Let him that thinketh he standeth take heed lest he fall." All need the help which God alone can give. Oh, how priceless is the sweet influence of the Spirit of God as it comes to depressed, despairing souls, encouraging the faint-hearted, strengthening the feeble, and imparting courage and help to the tried servants of the Lord! Oh, what a God is ours, who deals gently with the erring, and manifests his patience and tenderness when we are in adversity, and when we are overwhelmed with some great sorrow!

David ought not to have distrusted God for one moment. Wherever the children of God make a failure, it is due to their lack of faith. When shadows encompass the soul, when we want light and guidance, we must look up; there is light beyond the darkness. We must learn to trust our heavenly Father, and not allow the soul to be defiled with the sin of unbelief. In trying to save ourselves, we do not commit the keeping of our souls to God, as unto a faithful Creator. We do not expect him to work for us, but frantically beat about in our own finite strength to break through some wall of difficulty which God alone can remove for us. Man is nothing without God. The example of the good and noble men of sacred history, is to be imitated by us only where they followed the footsteps of the Lord. When man relies implicitly upon God, he will be true to himself; and he can hope and rejoice in the God of his salvation, though every friend of earth becomes a foe.

David had reason to trust God. He was the Lord's anointed. He had been protected in the midst of danger by the angels of God. He had been armed with valor and courage to do wonderful things, and if he had but removed his mind from the distressing situation in which he was placed, and thought of God's wonderful power and majesty, he would have been at peace even in the midst of the shadows of death, and could with confidence have repeated the promise of the Lord, "The mountains shall depart, and the hills be removed; but my kindness shall not depart from thee, neither shall the covenant of my peace be removed, saith the Lord that hath mercy on thee." *Signs of the Times,* August 31, 1888.

David's Family Reunited

Among the mountains of Judah, David sought refuge from the pursuit of Saul. He made good his escape to the cave of Adullam, a place that, with a small force, could be held against a large army. "And when his brethren and all his father's house heard it, they went down thither to him." The family of David could not feel secure, knowing that at any time the unreasonable suspicions of Saul might be directed against them on account of their relation to David. They had now learned—what was coming to be generally known in Israel—that God had chosen David as the future ruler of His people; and they believed that they would be safer with him, even though he was a fugitive in a lonely cave, than they could be while exposed to the insane madness of a jealous king.

In the cave of Adullam the family were united in sympathy and affection. The son of Jesse could make melody with voice and harp as he sang, "Behold, how good and how pleasant it is for brethren to dwell together in unity!" Psalm 133:1. He had tasted the bitterness of distrust on the part of his own brothers; and the harmony that had taken the place of discord brought joy to the exile's heart. It was here that David composed the fifty-seventh psalm.

It was not long before David's company was joined by others who desired to escape the exactions of the king. There were many who had lost confidence in the ruler of Israel, for they could see that he was no longer guided by the Spirit of the Lord. "And everyone that was in distress, and everyone that was in debt, and everyone that was discontented," resorted to David, "and he became a captain over them: and there were with him about four hundred men." Here David had a little kingdom of his own, and in it order and discipline prevailed. But even in his retreat in the mountains he was far from feeling secure, for he received continual evidence that the king had not relinquished his murderous purpose. *Patriarchs and Prophets*, 657, 658.

Stern Self-Discipline

When by the jealousy of Saul driven a fugitive into the wilderness, David, cut off from human support, leaned more heavily upon God. The uncertainty and unrest of the wilderness life, its unceasing peril, its necessity for frequent flight, the character of the men who gathered to him there, — "everyone that was in distress, and everyone that was in debt, and everyone that was discontented" (1 Samuel 22:2),—all rendered the more essential a stern self-discipline. These experiences aroused and developed power to deal with men, sympathy for the oppressed, and hatred of injustice. Through years of waiting and peril, David learned to find in God his comfort, his support, his life. He learned that only by God's power could he come to the throne; only in His wisdom could he rule wisely. It was through the training in the school of hardship and sorrow that David was able to make the record—though afterward marred with his great sin—that he "executed judgment and justice unto all his people." 2 Samuel 8:15. *Education,* 152.

He found a refuge for his parents with the king of Moab, and then, at a warning of danger from a prophet of the Lord, he fled from his hiding place to the forest of Hareth. The experience through which David was passing was not unnecessary or fruitless. God was giving him a course of discipline to fit him to become a wise general as well as a just and merciful king. With his band of fugitives he was gaining a preparation to take up the work that Saul, because of his murderous passion and blind indiscretion, was becoming wholly unfitted to do. Men cannot depart from the counsel of God and still retain that calmness and wisdom which will enable them to act with justice and discretion. There is no insanity so dreadful, so hopeless, as that of following human wisdom, unguided by the wisdom of God.

Saul had been preparing to ensnare and capture David in the cave of Adullam, and when it was discovered that David had left this place of refuge, the king was greatly enraged. The flight of David was a mystery to Saul. He could account for it only by the belief that there had been traitors in his camp, who had informed the son of Jesse of his proximity and design.

He affirmed to his counselors that a conspiracy had been formed against him, and with the offer of rich gifts and positions of honor he bribed them to reveal who among his people had befriended David. *Patriarchs and Prophets,* 658, 659.

Doeg Misrepresents David and Ahimelech

When Doeg the Edomite heard the words of Saul offering as a bribe the gift of vineyards, and the position of captain over thousands and hundreds, his ambition was stirred, and he determined to turn informer. He had been at Nob and had witnessed the action of the priest [Ahimelech] when he provided David with bread, and gave him the sword of Goliath. He cherished hatred toward the man in holy office, because he had reproved him for his sins; and now a favorable opportunity presented itself, not only to gain riches and position, but to be avenged on the priest. *Signs of the Times*, September 21, 1888.

Moved by ambition and avarice, and by hatred of the priest, who had reproved his sins, Doeg reported David's visit to Ahimelech, representing the matter in such a light as to kindle Saul's anger against the man of God. The words of that mischievous tongue, set on fire of hell, stirred up the worst passions in Saul's heart. Maddened with rage, he declared that the whole family of the priest should perish. And the terrible decree was executed. Not only Ahimelech, but the members of his father's house— "fourscore and five persons that did wear a linen ephod" —were slain at the king's command, by the murderous hand of Doeg. *Patriarchs and Prophets*, 659.

David's Remorse

After the slaughter of the priests, "one of the sons of Ahimelech the son of Ahitub, named Abiathar, escaped, and fled after David. And Abiathar showed David that Saul had slain the Lord's priests. And David said unto Abiathar, I knew it that day, when Doeg the Edomite was there, that he would surely tell Saul; I have occasioned the death of all the persons of thy father's house. Abide thou with me, fear not; for he that seeketh my life seeketh thy life; but with me thou shalt be in safeguard." *Signs of the Times*, October 5, 1888.

David Rescues Keilah

While David was in his refuge in the forests of Hareth, he was informed that the Philistines were warring against the men of Keilah, and that the people were in great distress, for their enemies were robbing the threshing-floors. "Therefore David inquired of the Lord, saying, Shall I go and smite these Philistines? And the Lord said unto David, Go, and smite the Philistines, and save Keilah. And David's men said unto him, Behold, we be afraid here in Judah; how much more then if we come to Keilah against the armies of the Philistines." The men who had cast in their lot with David, looked at their small force, —only a few hundred men, —and they were filled with dread at the thought of an encounter with the superior numbers of their enemies. They were also afraid that Saul would attack them, and that between the two armies they would be overwhelmed.

> *He had been anointed as king, and he thought that some measure of responsibility rested upon him for the protection of his people*

David again sought the Lord. It was the manifest fear and reluctance of his men that led him again to inquire of the Lord. He had been anointed as king, and he thought that some measure of responsibility rested upon him for the protection of his people. If he could but have the positive assurance that he was moving in the path of duty, he would start out with his limited forces, and stand faithfully at his post whatever might be the consequences. David was well aware that while Saul was occupied almost entirely with planning and with executing his plans for his discovery and capture, he could not be strengthening his kingdom, or promoting the good of his subjects.

The people of Keilah were being grievously oppressed, for, while their enemies were encamped without their walls, they were being robbed of the necessities of life. In answer to the inquiry of David, the Lord said, "Arise, go down to Keilah; for I will deliver the Philistines into thine hand. So David and his men went to Keilah, and fought with the Philistines, and brought away their cattle, and smote them with a great slaughter. So David saved the inhabitants of Keilah." *Signs of the Times,* October 5, 1888.

David Faces Ingratitude

Still hunted by the king, David found no place of rest or security. At Keilah his brave band saved the town from capture by the Philistines, but they were not safe, even among the people whom they had delivered. From Keilah they repaired to the wilderness of Ziph. *Patriarchs and Prophets,* 660.

The citizens of Keilah, who should have repaid the interest and zeal of David in delivering them from the hands of the Philistines, would have given him up because of their fear of Saul rather than to have suffered a siege for his sake. But the men of Ziph would do worse; they would betray David into the hands of his enemy, not because of their loyalty to the king, but because of their hatred of David. Their interest for the king was only a pretense. They were of their own accord acting the part of hypocrites when they offered to assist in the capture of David. It was upon these false-hearted betrayers that Saul invoked the blessing of the Lord. He praised their satanic spirit in betraying an innocent man, as the spirit and act of virtue in showing compassion to himself. Apparently David was in greater danger than he had ever been before. Upon learning the perils to which he was exposed, he changed his position, seeking refuge in the mountains between Maon and the Dead Sea. *SDA Bible Commentaries,* vol. 2, 1021.

Jonathan Encourages David

At this time, when there were so few bright spots in the path of David, he was rejoiced to receive an unexpected visit from Jonathan, who had learned the place of his refuge. Precious were the moments which these two friends passed in each other's society. They related their varied experiences, and Jonathan strengthened the heart of David, saying, "Fear not: for the hand of Saul my father shall not find thee; and thou shalt be king over Israel, and I shall be next unto thee; and that also Saul my father knoweth." As they talked of the wonderful dealings of God with David, the hunted fugitive was greatly encouraged. "And they two made a covenant before the Lord: and David abode in the wood, and Jonathan went to his house."

After the visit of Jonathan, David encouraged his soul with songs of praise, accompanying his voice with his harp as he sang:

"In the Lord put I my trust:

How say ye to my soul,

Flee as a bird to your mountain?

For, lo, the wicked bend their bow,

They make ready their arrow upon the string,

That they may privily shoot at the upright in heart.

If the foundations be destroyed, What can the righteous do?

The Lord is in His holy temple,

The Lord's throne is in heaven:

His eyes behold, His eyelids try, the children of men.

The Lord trieth the righteous:

But the wicked and him that loveth violence His soul hateth."

Psalm 11:1–5. *Patriarchs and Prophets*, 660.

David's Conscience Spares Saul

Again word was sent to Saul, "Behold, David is in the wilderness of Engedi. Then Saul took three thousand chosen men out of all Israel, and went to seek David and his men upon the rocks of the wild goats." David had only six hundred men in his company, while Saul advanced against him with an army of three thousand. In a secluded cave the son of Jesse and his men waited for the guidance of God as to what should be done. As Saul was pressing his way up the mountains, he turned aside, and entered, alone, the very cavern in which David and his band were hidden. When David's men saw this they urged their leader to kill Saul. The fact that the king was now in their power was interpreted by them as certain evidence that God Himself had delivered the enemy into their hand, that they might destroy him. David was tempted to take this view of the matter; but the voice of conscience spoke to him, saying, "Touch not the anointed of the Lord." *Patriarchs and Prophets*, 661.

David Rules His Own Spirit

The course of David made it manifest that he had a Ruler whom he obeyed. He could not permit his natural passions to gain the victory over him; for he knew that he that ruleth his own spirit, is greater than he who taketh a city. If he had been led and controlled by human feelings, he would have reasoned that the Lord had brought his enemy under his power in order that he might slay him, and take the government of Israel upon himself. Saul's mind was in such a condition that his authority was not respected, and the people were becoming irreligious and demoralized. Yet the fact that Saul had been divinely chosen king of Israel kept him in safety, for David conscientiously served God, and he would not in any wise harm the anointed of the Lord. David's men could scarcely consent to leave Saul in peace, and they said to their commander, "Behold the day of which the Lord said unto thee, Behold, I will deliver thine enemy into thine hand, that thou mayest do to him as it shall seem good unto thee. Then David arose, and cut off the skirt of Saul's robe privily." But his tender conscience smote him afterward, because he had marred the garment of the king.

Saul rose up and went out of the cave to continue his search after David. But a voice fell upon his startled ears, saying, "My lord the king." He turned to see who was addressing him, and lo! it was the son of Jesse, the man whom he had so long desired to have in his power that he might kill him. David bowed himself to the king, acknowledging him as his master. David addressed Saul in these words: "Wherefore hearest thou men's words, saying, Behold, David seeketh thy hurt? Behold, this day thine eyes have seen how that the Lord had delivered thee today into mine hand in the cave; and some bade me kill thee; but mine eye spared thee; and I said, I will not put forth mine hand against my lord; for he is the Lord's anointed. Moreover, my father, see, yea, see the skirt of thy robe in my hand; for in that I cut off the skirt of thy robe, and killed thee not, know thou and see that there is neither evil nor transgression in mine hand, and I have not sinned against thee; yet thou huntest my soul to take it. The Lord judge between me and thee, and the Lord avenge me of thee; but mine hand shall not be upon thee." *Signs of the Times*, October 12, 1888.

David Kind, but Wary

When Saul heard the words of David he was humbled, and could not but admit their truthfulness. His feelings were deeply moved as he realized how completely he had been in the power of the man whose life he sought. David stood before him in conscious innocence. With a softened spirit, Saul exclaimed, "Is this thy voice, my son David? And Saul lifted up his voice, and wept." Then he declared to David: "Thou art more righteous than I: for thou hast rewarded me good, whereas I have rewarded thee evil … For if a man find his enemy, will he let him go well away? wherefore the Lord reward thee good for that thou hast done unto me this day. And now, behold, I know well that thou shalt surely be king, and that the kingdom of Israel shall be established in thine hand." And David made a covenant with Saul that when this should take place he would favorably regard the house of Saul, and not cut off his name. Knowing what he did of Saul's past course, David could put no confidence in the assurances of the king, nor hope that his penitent condition would long continue. So when Saul returned to his home David remained in the strongholds of the mountains. *Patriarchs and Prophets*, 662.

> *David could put no confidence in the assurances of the king, nor hope that his penitent condition would long continue*

Tender and Courteous—A Lesson for All

The conduct of David toward Saul has a lesson. By command of God, Saul had been anointed as king over Israel. Because of his disobedience the Lord declared that the kingdom should be taken from him; and yet how tender and courteous and forbearing was the conduct of David toward him! In seeking the life of David, Saul came into the wilderness and, unattended, entered the very cave where David with his men of war lay hidden. "And the men of David said unto him, Behold the day of which the Lord said unto thee, ... I will deliver thine enemy into thine hand, that thou mayest do to him as it shall seem good unto thee. And he said unto his men, The Lord forbid that I should do this thing unto my master, the Lord's anointed, to stretch forth mine hand against him, seeing he is the anointed of the Lord." The Saviour bids us, "Judge not, that ye be not judged. For with what judgment ye judge, ye shall be judged: and with what measure ye mete, it shall be measured to you again." Remember that soon your life record will pass in review before God. Remember, too, that He has said, "Thou art inexcusable, O man, whosoever thou art that judgest: for thou that judgest doest the same things." 1 Samuel 24:4–6; Matthew 7:1, 2; Romans 2:1. *Ministry of Healing,* 484.

David Mourns for Samuel

It was while Israel was racked with perplexity and internal strife, at a time when it seemed that the calm, God-fearing counsel of Samuel was most needed, that God gave his aged servant rest. Oh, how bitter were the reflections of Israel as they looked upon his quiet resting-place, and remembered their folly in rejecting him as their ruler; for he had had so close a connection with Heaven that he seemed to bind all Israel to the throne of Jehovah. It was Samuel who had taught them to love and obey God; but now that he was dead, the people felt that they were to be left to the mercies of a king who was joined to Satan, and who would divorce the people from God and Heaven. *Signs of the Times,* October 19, 1888.

David could not be present at the burial of Samuel, but he mourned for him as deeply and tenderly as a faithful son could mourn for a devoted father. He knew that Samuel's death had broken another bond of restraint from the actions of Saul, and he felt less secure than when the prophet lived. While the attention of Saul was engaged in mourning for the death of Samuel, David took the opportunity to seek a place of greater security; so he fled to the wilderness of Paran. It was here that he composed the one hundred and twentieth and twenty-first psalms. In these desolate wilds, realizing that the prophet was dead, and the king was his enemy, he sang:

"My help cometh from the Lord, Which made heaven and earth.

He will not suffer thy foot to be moved: He that keepeth thee will not slumber. Behold, He that keepeth Israel

Shall neither slumber nor sleep...

The Lord shall preserve thee from all evil: He shall preserve thy soul.

The Lord shall preserve thy going out and thy coming in

From this time forth, and even forevermore." Psalm 121:2–8. *Patriarchs and Prophets*, 664.

Nabal Offends David

While David and his men were in the wilderness of Paran, they protected from the depredations of marauders the flocks and herds of a wealthy man named Nabal, who had vast possessions in that region. Nabal was a descendant of Caleb, but his character was churlish and niggardly. *Patriarchs and Prophets*, 664.

David and his men were in sore need of provisions while at this place, and when the son of Jesse heard that Nabal was shearing his sheep he sent out ten young men, and David said unto the young men, "Get you up to Carmel, and go to Nabal, and greet him in my name; and thus shall ye say to him that liveth in prosperity, Peace be both to thee, and peace be to thine house, and peace be unto all that thou hast. And now I have heard that thou hast shearers; now thy shepherds which were with us, we hurt them not, neither was there aught missing unto them, all the while they were in Carmel. Ask thy young men, and they will show thee. Wherefore let the young men find favor in thine eyes; for we come in a good day; give, I pray thee, whatsoever cometh to thine hand unto thy servants, and to thy son David."

David and his men had been like a wall of protection to the shepherds and flocks of Nabal as they pastured in the mountains.

And he courteously petitioned that supplies be given them in their great need from the abundance of this rich man. They might have helped themselves from the flocks and herds; but they did not. They behaved themselves in an honest way; but their kindness was all lost upon Nabal. The answer he returned to David was indicative of his character. "And Nabal answered David's servants, and said, Who is David? and who is the son of Jesse? there be many servants nowadays that break away every man from his master. Shall I then take my bread, and my water, and my flesh that I have killed for my shearers, and give it unto men, whom I know not whence they be?" When the young men returned empty-handed, disappointed and disgusted, and related the affair to David, he was filled with indignation. "Surely," he said, "in vain have I kept all that this fellow hath in the wilderness, so that nothing was missed of all that pertained unto him; and he has requited me evil for good." David commanded his men to gird on their swords, and equip themselves for an encounter; for he had determined to punish the man who had denied him what was his right, and had added insult to injury. This impulsive movement was more in harmony with the manner of Saul than with that of David, but the son of Jesse had yet to learn lessons of patience in the school of affliction. *Signs of the Times*, October 26, 1888.

The Lord would have the wife render respect unto her husband, but always as it is fit in the Lord. In the character of Abigail, the wife of Nabal, we have an illustration of womanhood after the order of Christ, while her husband illustrates what a man may become who yields himself to the control of Satan. When David was a fugitive from the face of Saul, he had camped near the possessions of Nabal and had protected the flocks and the shepherds of this man from all depredation while in Carmel.

In a time of need David sent messengers to Nabal with a courteous message, asking for food for himself and his men, and Nabal answered with insolence, returning evil for good, and refusing to share his abundance with his neighbors. No message could have been more respectful than that which David sent to this man, but Nabal accused David and his men falsely in order to justify himself in his selfishness, and represented David and his followers as runaway slaves. When the messenger returned with this insolent taunt, David's indignation was aroused, and he determined to have speedy revenge. *Manuscript Releases,* vol. 21, 213.

David's Impulsiveness

When the young men returned empty-handed and related the affair to David, he was filled with indignation. He commanded his men to equip themselves for an encounter; for he had determined to punish the man who had denied him what was his right, and had added insult to injury. This impulsive movement was more in harmony with the character of Saul than with that of David, but the son of Jesse had yet to learn of patience in the school of affliction.

> *This impulsive movement was more in harmony with the character of Saul than with that of David, but the son of Jesse had yet to learn of patience in the school of affliction*

One of Nabal's servants hastened to Abigail, the wife of Nabal, after he had dismissed David's young men, and told her what had happened. "Behold," he said, "David sent messengers out of the wilderness to salute our master; and he railed on them. But the men were very good unto us, and we were not hurt, neither missed we anything, as long as we were conversant with them, when we were in the fields. They were a wall unto us both by night and day, all the while we were with them keeping the sheep. Now therefore know and consider what thou wilt do; for evil is determined against our master, and against all his household." *Patriarchs and Prophets,* 665.

Abigail Soothes David's Irritation

Abigail saw that something must be done to avert the result of Nabal's fault, and that she must take the responsibility of acting immediately without the counsel of her husband. She knew that it would be useless to speak to him, for he would only receive her proposition with abuse and contempt. He would remind her that he was the lord of his household, that she was his wife and therefore in subjection to him, and must do as he should dictate.

She knew that the evil message must be counteracted immediately, and, without his consent, she gathered together such stores as she thought best to conciliate the wrath of David, for she knew he was determined to avenge himself for the insult he had received. She knew also that Nabal was so set and determined in his way that he would never consent to receive her counsel or act upon her plan. She herself brought to David the things that Nabal had refused to give, and bound herself to David's cause for his own good. Abigail's course in this matter was one that God approved, and the circumstance revealed in her a noble spirit and character. *Manuscript Releases,* vol. 21, 213.

With kind words she sought to soothe his irritated feelings, and she pleaded with him in behalf of her husband. With nothing of ostentation or pride, but full of the wisdom and love of God, Abigail revealed the strength of her devotion to her household; and she made it plain to David that the unkind course of her husband was in no wise premeditated against him as a personal affront, but was simply the outburst of an unhappy and selfish nature. *Patriarchs and Prophets,* 666.

These words could only have come from the lips of one who had partaken of that wisdom which cometh down from above. The piety of Abigail, like the fragrance of a flower, breathed out all unconsciously in face and word and action. The Spirit of the Son of God was abiding in her soul. Her heart was full of purity, gentleness, and sanctified love. Her speech, seasoned with grace, and full of kindness and peace, shed a heavenly influence. Better impulses came to David, and he trembled as he thought what might have been the consequences of his rash purpose. An entire household would have been slain, containing more than one precious, God-fearing person like Abigail, who had engaged in the blessed ministry of good. Her words healed the sore and bruised heart of David. Would that there were more women who would soothe the irritated feelings, prevent rash impulses, and quell great evils by words of calm and well-directed wisdom. "Blessed are the peacemakers; for they shall be called the children of God." *Signs of the Times*, October 26, 1888.

David Escapes Disgrace

Abigail rejoiced that her mission had been successful, and that she had been instrumental in saving her household from death. David rejoiced that through her timely advice he had been prevented from committing deeds of violence and revenge. Upon reflection, he realized that it would have been a matter of disgrace to him before Israel, and a remembrance that would always have caused him the keenest remorse. He felt that he and his men had the greatest cause for gratitude. He had had a horror of bloodshed, and had prayed that he might be delivered from blood guiltiness; and yet, when his feelings were injured, he had planned to avenge himself with his own hands. In this he had taken it upon himself to act in the place of God, who has said, "Vengeance is mine, I will repay."

David had taken an oath that Nabal and his household should perish; but now he saw that it was not only wrong to make such a vow, but it would be wrong to keep it. If Herod had had the moral courage of David, no matter how humiliating it might have been, he would have retracted the oath that devoted John the Baptist's head to the ax of the executioner, that the revenge of an evil woman might be accomplished, and he would not have had upon his soul the guilt of the murder of the prophet of God. *Signs of the Times*, October 26, 1888.

A consecrated Christian life is ever shedding light and comfort and peace. It is characterized by purity, tact, simplicity, and usefulness. It is controlled by that unselfish love that sanctifies the influence. It is full of Christ, and leaves a track of light wherever its possessor may go. Abigail was a wise reprover and counselor. David's passion died away under the power of her influence and reasoning. He was convinced that he had taken an unwise course and had lost control of his own spirit. *Patriarchs and Prophets*, 667.

When David heard the tidings of the death of Nabal, he gave thanks that God had taken vengeance into his own hands. He had been restrained from evil, and the Lord had returned the wickedness of the wicked upon his own head. In this dealing of God with Nabal and David, men may be encouraged to put their cases into the hands of God; for in his own good time he will set matters right.

David's Mistake of Polygamy

David afterward married Abigail. This was not according to the original plan of God; it was in direct opposition to his design, that a man should have more than one wife. David was already the husband of Ahinoam. The gospel condemns the practice of polygamy. The custom of the nations of David's time had perverted his judgment and influenced his actions. Great men have erred greatly in following the practices of the world. The study of everyone should be to know what is the will of God and what saith the word of the Lord. The bitter result of this practice of marrying many wives was permitted to be sorely felt throughout all the life of David. *Signs of the Times*, October 26, 1888.

Saul's Life Spared by David

After the death of Samuel, David was left in peace for a few months. Again he repaired to the solitude of the Ziphites; but these enemies, hoping to secure the favor of the king, informed him of David's hiding place. This intelligence aroused the demon of passion that had been slumbering in Saul's breast. Once more he summoned his men of arms and led them out in pursuit of David. But friendly spies brought tidings to the son of Jesse that Saul was again pursuing him; and with a few of his men, David started out to learn the location of his enemy. It was night when, cautiously advancing, they came upon the encampment, and saw before them the tents of the king and his attendants. They were unobserved, for the camp was quiet in slumber. David called upon his friends to go with him into the very midst of the foe. In answer to his question, "Who will go down with me to Saul to the camp?" Abishai promptly responded, "I will go down with thee."

Hidden by the deep shadows of the hills, David and his attendant entered the encampment of the enemy. As they sought to ascertain the exact number of their foes, they came upon Saul sleeping, his spear stuck in the ground, and a cruse of water at his head. Beside him lay Abner, his chief commander, and all around them were the soldiers, locked in slumber. Abishai raised his spear, and said to David, "God hath delivered thine enemy into thine hand this day: now therefore let me smite him, I pray thee, with the spear even to the earth at once, and I will not smite him the second time." He waited for the word of permission; but there fell upon his ear the whispered words: "Destroy him not: for who can stretch forth his hand against the Lord's anointed, and be guiltless? ... As the Lord liveth, the Lord shall smite him; or his day shall come to die; or he shall descend into battle, and perish. The Lord forbid that I should stretch forth mine hand against the Lord's anointed:

but, I pray thee, take thou now the spear that is at his bolster, and the cruse of water, and let us go. So David took the spear and the cruse of water from Saul's bolster; and they gat them away, and no man saw it, nor knew it, neither awaked: for they were all asleep; because a deep sleep from the Lord was fallen upon them." How easily the Lord can weaken the strongest, remove prudence from the wisest, and baffle the skill of the most watchful!

When David was at a safe distance from the camp he stood on the top of a hill and cried with a loud voice to the people and to Abner, saying, "Art not thou a valiant man? and who is like to thee in Israel? wherefore then hast thou not kept thy lord the king? for there came one of the people in to destroy the king thy lord. This thing is not good that thou hast done. As the Lord liveth, ye are worthy to die, because ye have not kept your master the Lord's anointed. And now see where the king's spear is, and the cruse of water that was at his bolster. And Saul knew David's voice, and said, Is this thy voice, my son David? And David said, It is my voice, my lord, O king. And he said, Wherefore doth my lord thus pursue after his servant? for what have I done? or what evil is in mine hand? Now therefore, I pray thee, let my lord the king hear the words of his servant." Again the acknowledgment fell from the lips of the king, "I have sinned: return, my son David; for I will no more do thee harm, because my soul was precious in thine eyes this day: behold, I have played the fool, and have erred exceedingly. And David answered and said, Behold the king's spear! and let one of the young men come over and fetch it." Although Saul had made the promise, "I will no more do thee harm," David did not place himself in his power. *Patriarchs and Prophets*, 668–671.

Saul had meant all that he had said, yet his relenting and confession came not from genuine repentance and conversion of heart. *Signs of the Times*, November 2, 1888.

A Lack of Faith Displayed

David despaired of a reconciliation with Saul. It seemed inevitable that he should at last fall a victim to the malice of the king, and he determined again to seek refuge in the land of the Philistines. With the six hundred men under his command, he passed over to Achish, the king of Gath.

David's conclusion that Saul would certainly accomplish his murderous purpose was formed without the counsel of God. Even while Saul was plotting and seeking to accomplish his destruction, the Lord was working to secure David the kingdom. God works out His plans, though to human eyes they are veiled in mystery. Men cannot understand the ways of God; and, looking at appearances, they interpret the trials and tests and provings that God permits to come upon them as things that are against them, and that will only work their ruin. Thus David looked on appearances, and not at the promises of God. He doubted that he would ever come to the throne. Long trials had wearied his faith and exhausted his patience.

> *Men cannot understand the ways of God; and, looking at appearances, they interpret the trials and tests and provings that God permits to come upon them as things that are against them, and that will only work their ruin*

The Lord did not send David for protection to the Philistines, the most bitter foes of Israel. This very nation would be among his worst enemies to the last, and yet he had fled to them for help in his time of need. Having lost all confidence in Saul and in those who served him, he threw himself upon the mercies of the enemies of his people. David was a brave general, and had proved himself a wise and successful warrior; but he was working directly against his own interests when he went to the Philistines. God had appointed him to set up his standard in the land of Judah, and it was want of faith that led him to forsake his post of duty without a command from the Lord.

God was dishonored by David's unbelief. The Philistines had feared David more than they had feared Saul and his armies; and by placing himself under the protection of the Philistines, David discovered to them the weakness of his own people. Thus he encouraged these relentless foes to oppress Israel. David had been anointed to stand in defense of the people of God; and the Lord would not have His servants give encouragement to the wicked by disclosing the weakness of His people or by an appearance of indifference to their welfare. Furthermore, the impression was received by his brethren that he had gone to the heathen to serve their gods. By this act he gave occasion for misconstruing his motives, and many were led to hold prejudice against him. The very thing that Satan desired to have him do he was led to do; for, in seeking refuge among the Philistines, David caused great exultation to the enemies of God and His people. David did not renounce his worship of God nor cease his devotion to His cause; but he sacrificed his trust in Him to his personal safety, and thus tarnished the upright and faithful character that God requires His servants to possess. *Patriarchs and Prophets*, 672.

David was cordially received at Gath by the king of the Philistines. The warmth of his reception was partly due to the fact that the king admired him, and partly to the fact that it was flattering to his vanity to have a Hebrew leave his own nation to seek his protection. Achish hoped to be successful not only in gaining David as an ally, but in gaining others also, for he felt assured that many would be influenced through David's example to rally under his standard. David felt secure from betrayal in the dominions of Achish. He brought his family, his household, and his possessions, as did also his men, and to all appearances he had come to locate permanently in the land of Philistia. All this was very gratifying to Achish, who solemnly promised to protect the fugitive Israelites.

At David's request for a residence in the country removed from the royal city, the king graciously granted Ziklag as a possession, and it was afterward annexed to Israel's dominions. For a year and six months, David made his home in the country of the Philistines. He had tasted the bitterness of envy at Saul's court, and he feared that he might have a similar experience in the court at Gath. But it was for far weightier reasons that he desired to leave the royal city. He realized that it would be dangerous for himself and [his] men to be under the influence of those who were connected with idolatry and transgression. In a town wholly separated for their use, they might worship God with more freedom than they could if they remained in Gath, where the senseless, heathen rites could but prove a source of evil and annoyance.

David's Deception

While dwelling in this isolated town, David made war upon the Geshurites, the Gezrites, and the Amalekites, and he left neither man nor woman alive to bring tidings to Gath. When he returned from battle, Achish inquired as to where he had been, and David gave him to understand that he had been warring against those of his own nation, the men of Judah. But by this very dissembling, he was the means of strengthening the hand of the Philistines, for the king said, "He hath made his people Israel utterly to abhor him; therefore he shall be my servant forever." *Signs of the Times*, November 16, 1888.

David knew that it was the will of God that those heathen tribes should be destroyed, and he knew that he was appointed to do this work; but he was not walking in the counsel of God when he practiced deception.

"And it came to pass in those days, that the Philistines gathered their armies together for warfare, to fight with Israel. And Achish said unto David, Know thou assuredly, that thou shalt go out with me to battle, thou and thy men." David had no intention of lifting his hand against his people; but he was not certain as to what course he would pursue, until circumstances should indicate his duty. He answered the king evasively, and said, "Surely thou shalt know what thy servant can do." Achish understood these words as a promise of assistance in the approaching war, and pledged his word to bestow upon David great honor, and give him a high position at the Philistine court. *Patriarchs and Prophets*, 673, 674.

David Resists Temptation

But although David's faith had staggered somewhat at the promises of God, he still remembered that Samuel had anointed him king of Israel. He recalled the victories that God had given him over his enemies in the past. He reviewed the great mercies of God in preserving him from the hand of Saul, and he determined that he would not betray any sacred trust, or imperil his soul's salvation. He would not join his forces with the enemy against Saul, even though the king had sought his life.

How many would have yielded to the temptation that Achish presented to David! How many have fallen, and how many will fall, into the snare of Satan for temporary advantages! Ambitious for exaltation, they will unite their influence with the avowed enemies of God's truth if they can only be honored among those who are honored of men. For present advantages, they will sacrifice the eternal good that God has in store for them. They will not endure the proving of God, and show themselves true in every place, and under all circumstances. God has promised that his faithful, obedient servants shall be exalted to be priests and kings. "Do ye not know that the saints shall judge the world?" *Signs of the Times*, November 16, 1888.

David's Predicament

David and his men had not taken part in the battle between Saul and the Philistines, though they had marched with the Philistines to the field of conflict. As the two armies prepared to join battle the son of Jesse found himself in a situation of great perplexity. It was expected that he would fight for the Philistines. Should he in the engagement quit the post assigned him and retire from the field, he would not only brand himself with cowardice, but with ingratitude and treachery to Achish, who had protected him and confided in him. Such an act would cover his name with infamy, and would expose him to the wrath of enemies more to be feared than Saul. Yet he could not for a moment consent to fight against Israel. Should he do this, he would become a traitor to his country—the enemy of God and of His people. It would forever bar his way to the throne of Israel; and should Saul be slain in the engagement, his death would be charged upon David.

David was caused to feel that he had missed his path. Far better would it have been for him to find refuge in God's strong fortresses of the mountains than with the avowed enemies of Jehovah and His people. But the Lord in His great mercy did not punish this error of His servant by leaving him to

> *But the Lord in His great mercy did not punish this error of His servant by leaving him to himself in his distress and perplexity; for though David, losing his grasp on divine power, had faltered and turned aside from the path of strict integrity, it was still the purpose of his heart to be true to God*

himself in his distress and perplexity; for though David, losing his grasp on divine power, had faltered and turned aside from the path of strict integrity, it was still the purpose of his heart to be true to God. While Satan and his host were busy helping the adversaries of God and of Israel to plan against a king who had forsaken God, the angels of the Lord were working to deliver David from the peril into which he had fallen. Heavenly messengers moved upon the Philistine princes to protest against the presence of David and his force with the army in the approachingconflict.

Thus Achish was forced to yield, and calling David, said unto him, "Surely as Jehovah liveth, thou hast been upright, and thy going out and thy coming in with me in the host is good in my sight: for I have not found evil in thee since the day of thy coming unto me unto this day. Nevertheless the lords favor thee not. Wherefore now return, and go in peace, that thou displease not the lords of the Philistines."

David, fearing to betray his real feelings, answered, "But what have I done? and what hast thou found in thy servant so long as I have been with thee unto this day, that I may not go fight against the enemies of my lord the king?"

The reply of Achish must have sent a thrill of shame and remorse through David's heart, as he thought how unworthy of a servant of Jehovah were the deceptions to which he had stooped. "I know that thou art good in my sight, as an angel of God," said the king: "notwithstanding, the princes of the Philistines have said, He shall not go up with us to the battle. Wherefore now rise up early in the morning with thy master's servants that are come with thee: and as soon as ye be up early in the morning, and have light, depart." Thus the snare in which David had become entangled was broken, and he was set free. *Patriarchs and Prophets*, 690, 691.

Ziklag Found Desolated

After three days' travel David and his band of six hundred men reached Ziklag, their Philistine home. But a scene of desolation met their view. The Amalekites, taking advantage of David's absence, with his force, had avenged themselves for his incursions into their territory. They had surprised the city while it was left unguarded, and having sacked and burned it, had departed, taking all the women and children as captives, with much spoil.

Dumb with horror and amazement, David and his men for a little time gazed in silence upon the blackened and smoldering ruins. Then as a sense of their terrible desolation burst upon them, those battle-scarred warriors "lifted up their voice and wept, until they had no more power to weep."

Here again David was chastened for the lack of faith that had led him to place himself among the Philistines. He had opportunity to see how much safety could be found among the foes of God and His people. David's followers turned upon him as the cause of their calamities. He had provoked the vengeance of the Amalekites by his attack upon them; yet, too confident of security in the midst of his enemies, he had left the city unguarded. Maddened with grief and rage, his soldiers were now ready for any desperate measures, and they threatened even to stone their leader.

Faith in Extremity

David seemed to be cut off from every human support. All that he held dear on earth had been swept from him. Saul had driven him from his country; the Philistines had driven him from the camp; the Amalekites had plundered his city; his wives and children had been made prisoners; and his own familiar friends had banded against him, and threatened him even with death. In this hour of utmost extremity David, instead of permitting his mind to dwell upon these painful circumstances, looked earnestly to God for help. He "encouraged himself in the Lord." He reviewed his past eventful life. Wherein had the Lord ever forsaken him? His soul was refreshed in recalling the many evidences of God's favor. The followers of David, by their discontent and impatience, made their affliction doubly grievous; but the man of God, having even greater cause for grief, bore himself with fortitude. "What time I am afraid, I will trust in Thee" (Psalm 56:3), was the language of his heart. Though he himself could not discern a way out of the difficulty, God could see it, and would teach him what to do.

Sending for Abiathar the priest, the son of Ahimelech, "David inquired of the Lord, saying, If I pursue after this troop, shall I overtake them?" The answer was, "Pursue: for thou shalt surely overtake them, and shalt without fail recover all." 1 Samuel 30:8, R.V.

At these words the tumult of grief and passion ceased. David and his soldiers at once set out in pursuit of their fleeing foe. So rapid was their march, that upon reaching the brook Besor, which empties near Gaza into the Mediterranean Sea, two hundred of the band were compelled by exhaustion to remain behind. But David with the remaining four hundred pressed forward, nothing daunted.

Advancing, they came upon an Egyptian slave apparently about to perish from weariness and hunger. Upon receiving food and drink, however, he revived, and they learned that he had been left to die by his cruel master, an Amalekite belonging to the invading force. He told the story of the raid and pillage; and then, having exacted a promise that he should not be slain or delivered to his master, he consented to lead David's company to the camp of their enemies.

As they came in sight of the encampment a scene of revelry met their gaze. The victorious host were holding high festival. "They were spread abroad upon all the earth, eating and drinking, and dancing, because of all the great spoil that they had taken out of the land of the Philistines, and out of the land of Judah." An immediate attack was ordered, and the pursuers rushed fiercely upon their prey. The Amalekites were surprised and thrown into confusion. The battle was continued all that night and the following day, until nearly the entire host was slain. Only a band of four hundred men, mounted upon camels, succeeded in making their escape. The word of the Lord was fulfilled. "David recovered all that the Amalekites had carried away: and David rescued his two wives. And there was nothing lacking to them, neither small nor great, neither sons nor daughters, neither spoil, nor anything that they had taken to them: David recovered all." *Patriarchs and Prophets*, 692, 693.

David's Spoil

Besides recovering all the spoil that had been taken from Ziklag, David and his band had captured extensive flocks and herds belonging to the Amalekites. These were called "David's spoil;" and upon returning to Ziklag, he sent from this spoil presents to the elders of his own tribe of Judah. In this distribution all those were remembered who had befriended him and his followers in the mountain fastnesses, when he had been forced to flee from place to place for his life. Their kindness and sympathy, so precious to the hunted fugitive, were thus gratefully acknowledged. *Patriarchs and Prophets*, 694.

David Mourns for Saul and Jonathan

It was the third day since David and his warriors returned to Ziklag. As they labored to restore their ruined homes, they watched with anxious hearts for tidings of the battle which they knew must have been fought between Israel and the Philistines. Suddenly a messenger entered the town, "with his clothes rent, and earth upon his head." He was at once brought to David, before whom he bowed with reverence, expressing recognition of him as a powerful prince, whose favor he desired. David eagerly inquired how the battle had gone. The fugitive reported Saul's defeat and death, and the death of Jonathan. But he went beyond a simple statement of facts. Evidently supposing that David must cherish enmity toward his relentless persecutor, the stranger hoped to secure honor to himself as the slayer of the king. With an air of boasting the man went on to relate that during the battle he found the monarch of Israel wounded, and sore pressed by his foes, and that at his own request the messenger had slain him. The crown from his head and the golden bracelets from his arm he had brought to David. He confidently expected that these tidings would be hailed with joy, and that a rich reward would be his for the part that he had acted.

But "David took hold on his clothes, and rent them; and likewise all the men that were with him: and they mourned, and wept, and fasted until even, for Saul, and for Jonathan his son, and for the people of the Lord, and for the house of Israel; because they were fallen by the sword." *Patriarchs and Prophets,* 694, 695.

David's grief at the death of Saul was sincere and deep, evincing the generosity of a noble nature. He did not exult in the fall of his enemy. The obstacle that had barred his access to the throne of Israel was removed, but at this he did not rejoice. Death had obliterated the remembrance of Saul's distrust and cruelty, and now nothing in his history was thought of but that which was noble and kingly. The name of Saul was linked with that of Jonathan, whose friendship had been so true and so unselfish.

Jonathan, by birth heir to the throne, yet knowing himself set aside by the divine decree; to his rival the most tender and faithful of friends, shielding David's life at the peril of his own; steadfast at his father's side through the dark days of his declining power, and at his side falling at the last—the name of Jonathan is treasured in heaven, and it stands on earth a witness to the existence and the power of unselfish love.

The song in which David gave utterance to the feelings of his heart became a treasure to his nation, and to the people of God in all subsequent ages: ...

> "How are the mighty fallen in the midst of the battle!
> Jonathan is slain upon thy high places.
> I am distressed for thee, my brother Jonathan:
> Very pleasant hast thou been unto me:
> Thy love to me was wonderful,
> Passing the love of women.
> How are the mighty fallen,
> And the weapons of war perished!" *Conflict and Courage,* 175.

Chapter Four

David Crowned King

The death of Saul removed the dangers that had made David an exile. The way was now open for him to return to his own land. When the days of mourning for Saul and Jonathan were ended, "David inquired of the Lord, saying, Shall I go up into any of the cities of Judah? And the Lord said unto him, Go up. And David said, Whither shall I go up? And He said, Unto Hebron." ...

David and his followers immediately prepared to obey the instruction which they had received from God. The six hundred armed men, with their wives and children, their flocks and herds, were soon on the way to Hebron. As the caravan entered the city the men of Judah were waiting to welcome David as the future king of Israel. Arrangements were at once made for his coronation. "And there they anointed David king over the house of Judah." But no effort was made to establish his authority by force over the other tribes.

> *As the caravan entered the city the men of Judah were waiting to welcome David as the future king of Israel*

One of the first acts of the new-crowned monarch was to express his tender regard for the memory of Saul and Jonathan. Upon learning of the brave deed of the men of Jabesh-gilead in rescuing the bodies of the fallen leaders and giving them honorable burial,

David sent an embassy to Jabesh with the message, "Blessed be ye of the Lord, that ye have showed this kindness unto your lord, even unto Saul, and have buried him. And now the Lord show kindness and truth unto you: and I also will requite you this kindness." And he announced his own accession to the throne of Judah and invited the allegiance of those who had proved themselves so truehearted.

The Philistines did not oppose the action of Judah in making David king. They had befriended him in his exile, in order to harass and weaken the kingdom of Saul, and now they hoped that because of their former kindness to David the extension of his power would, in the end, work to their advantage. But David's reign was not to be free from trouble. With his coronation began the dark record of conspiracy and rebellion. David did not sit upon a traitor's throne; God had chosen him to be king of Israel, and there had been no occasion for distrust or opposition. Yet hardly had his authority been acknowledged by the men of Judah, when through the influence of Abner, Ishbosheth, the son of Saul, was proclaimed king, and set upon a rival throne in Israel. *Patriarchs and Prophets*, 697, 698.

At last treachery overthrew the throne that malice and ambition had established. Abner, becoming incensed against the weak and incompetent Ishbosheth, deserted to David, with the offer to bring over to him all the tribes of Israel. His proposals were accepted by the king, and he was dismissed with honor to accomplish his purpose. But the favorable reception of so valiant and famed a warrior excited the jealousy of Joab, the commander-in-chief of David's army. There was a blood feud between Abner and Joab, the former having slain Asahel, Joab's brother, during the war between Israel and Judah. Now Joab, seeing an opportunity to avenge his brother's death and rid himself of a prospective rival, basely took occasion to waylay and murder Abner.

David, upon hearing of this treacherous assault, exclaimed, "I and my kingdom are guiltless before the Lord forever from the blood of Abner the son of Ner. Let it rest on the head of Joab;

and on all his father's house." In view of the unsettled state of the kingdom, and the power and position of the murderers—for Joab's brother Abishai had been united with him—David could not visit the crime with just retribution, yet he publicly manifested his abhorrence of the bloody deed. The burial of Abner was attended with public honors. The army, with Joab at their head, were required to take part in the services of mourning, with rent garments and clothed in sackcloth. The king manifested his grief by keeping a fast upon the day of burial; he followed the bier as chief mourner; and at the grave he pronounced an elegy which was a cutting rebuke of the murderers. "The king lamented over Abner, and said:

"Died Abner as a fool dieth? Thy hands were not bound, Nor thy feet put into fetters: As a man falleth before wicked men, So fellest thou."

David's magnanimous recognition of one who had been his bitter enemy won the confidence and admiration of all Israel. "All the people took notice of it, and it pleased them: as whatsoever the king did pleased all the people. For all the people and all Israel understood that day that it was not of the king to slay Abner the son of Ner." In the private circle of his trusted counselors and attendants the king spoke of the crime, and recognizing his own inability to punish the murderers as he desired, he left them to the justice of God: "Know ye not that there is a prince and a great man fallen this day in Israel? And I am this day weak, though anointed king; and these men the sons of Zeruiah be too hard for me: the Lord shall reward the doer of evil according to his wickedness." *Patriarchs and Prophets,* 699, 700.

After the death of Ishbosheth there was a general desire among the leading men of Israel that David should become king of all the tribes. "So all the elders of Israel came to the King to Hebron; and King David made a league with them in Hebron before the Lord." They assured the king that they recognized his divine appointment to the kingdom of Israel, and David was greatly pleased, for he knew that their hearts had been touched by the Spirit of the Lord, and their eyes had been enlightened to see light in God's light. He knew that the promises of God to him and to Israel would be fulfilled if they walked according to the counsel of the Lord. It was evident to his mind that the dealings of the Lord with him had prepared him for the duties and responsibilities of his office. Through the providence of God, the way had been opened for him to come to the throne of Israel. He had no personal ambition to gratify, for he had not sought the honor to which he had been brought.

More than eight thousand of the descendants of Aaron, and of the Levites, waited upon David. The great change in the sentiments of the people was marked and decisive. The revolution was quiet and dignified, befitting the great work they were doing. Nearly half a million souls, the former subjects of Saul, thronged Hebron. The very hills and valleys were alive with the multitudes. The hour for the coronation was appointed, and the man who had been expelled from the courts of Saul, who had fled to preserve his life to the mountains and hills, and to the caves of the earth, was about to receive the highest honor that can be conferred upon man by his brother man. David, the hero of the hour, was arrayed in the royal robe, while around him was a most imposing company. Priests and elders clothed in the garments of their sacred office, officers and soldiers with glittering spear and helmet, and strangers from long distances, stood to witness the coronation of the chosen king. The sacred oil was put upon the brow of David by the high priest, for the anointing by Samuel was a prophetic ceremony of what would take place at the inauguration of the king. The time had come, and David, by solemn rite, is consecrated by the nation to his office as God's appointed vicegerent. The scepter, a signal of

> *Saul had been after the heart of Israel, but David is a man after God's own heart*

royalty and power, is placed in his hands. The covenant is written of his righteous sovereignty, and the people give their pledges of loyalty. The diadem is placed upon his brow, and the coronation ceremony is over. Israel has a king by the appointment of God.

Saul had been after the heart of Israel, but David is a man after God's own heart. And now the procession moves toward the gate of the city with the highest enthusiasm, crying, "Long live king David." The musicians express the gladness of the hour by notes of joy with voice and instrument. When David is seated upon his throne, his subjects congratulate him that God has established him as the ruler of Israel, and they declare their joy in having such a king to reign over them. The ceremonies of the day were over, and he who had waited patiently on the Lord beheld the promise of God fulfilled. "And David went on, and grew great, and the Lord God of hosts was with him." *Signs of the Times*, June 15, 1888.

Jerusalem Becomes the Capital

As soon as David was established on the throne of Israel, he began to plan for a more appropriate position for the capital of his realm. Twenty miles from Hebron a place was selected as the future metropolis of the kingdom. Before Joshua had led the armies of Israel over Jordan to the promised possession, it had been called Salem. Near this place Abraham had proved his loyalty to God. He had prepared an altar, and had laid upon it his only son Isaac, in obedience to the command of the Lord. Here had been the home of Melchizedek, the priest of the most high God, nearly nine hundred years before the coronation of David. It held a central and elevated position in the country, and it was barricaded by an environment of hills. On the north rose Lebanon, with its snow-crowned summits. Away to the south stretched the Arabian desert, with its moving sands. To the west were the waters of the Mediterranean, and to the east were the Dead Sea and the river Jordan.

In order to secure this much-desired location, the Hebrews must dispossess a remnant of the old Canaanites. King David called for men to besiege and take the city of Jebus from their heathen enemies. A large force gathered at the command of the King, and David left his throne, and his armies surrounded and took the city, and the capital of Israel was moved to Jebus. This heathen name was changed to the City of David, and it was afterward called Jerusalem, and Mount Zion. "And David went on, and grew great, and the Lord God of hosts was with him." *Signs of the Times*, June 22, 1888.

The King's First Battle

When the Philistines heard that David had been anointed king over all the tribes of Israel, they "came up to seek David; and David heard of it, and went down to the hold." The Philistines marshaled an immense force, hoping again to bring Israel into subjection. They spread themselves in the valley of Rephaim. "David inquired of the Lord, saying, Shall I go up to the Philistines? wilt thou deliver them into my hand?" And the Lord bade David go up, and promised to deliver the Philistines into his hand.

King David asked counsel of the Lord in his extremity, and the Lord hearkened and heard, and answered his servant, and Israel was victorious. But the Philistines made a more decided display, that they might intimidate Israel. Their numbers were very great. Again David sought the Lord, and the great I AM became the general of the armies of Israel. God himself laid the plan of the attack. He instructed David, saying, "Thou shalt not go up; but fetch a compass behind them, and come upon them over against the mulberry trees. And let it be, when thou hearest the sound of a going in the top of the mulberry trees, that then thou shalt bestir thyself; for then shall the Lord go out before thee, to smite the host of the Philistines."

If David had chosen his own way, as did Saul, success would not have attended his warfare. But David did as the Lord had commanded, and he "smote the Philistines from Geba until thou come to Gazer." *Signs of the Times*, June 22, 1888.

Retrieving the Ark

Now that David was firmly established upon the throne and free from the invasions of foreign foes, he turned to the accomplishment of a cherished purpose—to bring up the ark of God to Jerusalem. For many years the ark had remained at Kirjath-jearim, nine miles distant; but it was fitting that the capital of the nation should be honored with the token of the divine Presence.

David summoned thirty thousand of the leading men of Israel, for it was his purpose to make the occasion a scene of great rejoicing and imposing display. The people responded gladly to the call. The high priest, with his brethren in sacred office and the princes and leading men of the tribes, assembled at Kirjath-jearim. David was aglow with holy zeal. The ark was brought out from the house of Abinadab and placed upon a new cart drawn by oxen, while two of the sons of Abinadab attended it.

The men of Israel followed with exultant shouts and songs of rejoicing, a multitude of voices joining in melody with the sound of musical instruments; "David and all the house of Israel played before the Lord ... on harps, and on psalteries, and on timbrels, and on cornets, and on cymbals." It had been long since Israel had witnessed such a scene of triumph. With solemn gladness the vast procession wound its way along the hills and valleys toward the Holy City.

But "when they came to Nachon's threshing floor, Uzzah put forth his hand to the ark of God, and took hold of it; for the oxen shook it. And the anger of the Lord was kindled against Uzzah, and God smote him there for his rashness; [MARGINAL READING] and there he died by the ark of God." A sudden terror fell upon the rejoicing throng. David was astonished and greatly alarmed, and in his heart he questioned the justice of God. He had been seeking to honor the ark as the symbol of the divine presence. Why, then, had that fearful judgment been sent to turn the season of gladness into an occasion of grief and mourning? Feeling that it would be unsafe to have the ark near him, David determined to let it remain where it was. A place was found for it nearby, at the house of Obed-edom the Gittite. *Patriarchs and Prophets*, 704, 705.

Uzzah was angry with the oxen, because they stumbled. He showed a manifest distrust of God, as though he who had brought the ark from the land of the Philistines, could not take care of it. Angels who attended the ark struck down Uzzah for presuming impatiently to put his hand upon the ark of God.

"And David was afraid of the Lord that day, and said, How shall the ark of the Lord come to me? So David would not remove the ark of the Lord unto him into the city of David; but David carried it aside into the house of Obed-edom, the Gittite." David knew that he was a sinful man; and he was afraid that, like Uzzah, he should in some way be presumptuous, and call forth the wrath of God upon himself. "And the ark of the Lord continued in the house of Obed-edom, the Gittite, three months; and the Lord blessed Obed-edom, and all his household."

God would teach his people that, while his ark was a terror and death to those who transgressed his commandments contained in it, it was also a blessing and strength to those who were obedient to his commandments. When David heard that the house of Obed-edom was greatly blessed, and that all that he had prospered, because of the ark of God, he was very anxious to bring it to his own city. But before David ventured to move the sacred ark, he sanctified himself to God, and also commanded that all the men highest in authority in the kingdom should keep themselves from all worldly business, and everything which would distract their minds from sacred devotion. Thus should they sanctify themselves for the purpose of conducting the sacred ark to the city of David. "So David went and brought up the ark of God from the house of Obed-edom into the city of David with gladness. And it was so, that when they that bare the ark of the Lord had gone six paces, he sacrificed oxen and fatlings." *Spirit of Prophecy*, vol. 1, 410.

David Dances Before the Lord

David laid off his kingly attire, and clothed himself with garments similar to the priests', which had never been worn before, that not the least impurity might be upon his clothing. Every six paces, they erected an altar and solemnly sacrificed to God. The special blessing of the Lord rested upon king David, who thus manifested before his people his exalted reverence for the ark of God. "And David danced before the Lord with all his might; and David was girded with a linen ephod. So David and all the house of Israel brought up the ark of the Lord with shouting, and with the sound of the trumpet. And as the ark of the Lord came into the city of David, Michal, Saul's daughter, looked through a window, and saw king David leaping and dancing before the Lord; and she despised him in her heart." *Spirit of Prophecy*, vol. 1, 411.

David's dancing in reverent joy before God has been cited by pleasure lovers in justification of the fashionable modern dance, but there is no ground for such an argument. In our day dancing is associated with folly and midnight reveling. Health and morals are sacrificed to pleasure. By the frequenters of the ballroom God is not an object of thought and reverence; prayer or the song of praise would be felt to be out of place in their assemblies. This test should be decisive. Amusements that have a tendency to weaken the love for sacred things and lessen our joy in the service of God are not to be sought by Christians. The music and dancing in joyful praise to God at the removal of the ark had not the faintest resemblance to the dissipation of modern dancing. The one tended to the remembrance of God and exalted His holy name. The other is a device of Satan to cause men to forget God and to dishonor Him. *Patriarchs and Prophets,* 707.

The dignity and pride of king Saul's daughter were shocked that king David should lay aside his garments of royalty, and his royal scepter, and be clothed with the simple linen garments worn by the priests. She thought that he was greatly dishonoring himself before the people of Israel. But God honored David in the sight of all Israel by letting his Spirit abide upon him. David humbled himself, but God exalted him. He sung in an inspired manner, playing upon the harp, producing the most enchanting music. He felt, in a small degree, that holy joy that all the saints will experience at the voice of God when their captivity is turned, and God makes a covenant of peace with all who have kept his commandments.

> *But God honored David in the sight of all Israel by letting his Spirit abide upon him. David humbled himself, but God exalted him*

"And they brought in the ark of the Lord, and set it in his place, in the midst of the tabernacle that David had pitched for it. And David offered burnt-offerings and peace-offerings before the Lord." *Spirit of Prophecy,* vol. 1, 412.

David felt that it was the service of God which Michal had despised and dishonored, and he sternly answered: "It was before the Lord, which chose me before thy father, and before all his house, to appoint me ruler over the people of the Lord, over Israel: therefore will I play before the Lord. And I will yet be more vile than thus, and will be base in mine own sight: and of the maidservants which thou hast spoken of, of them shall I be had in honor." To David's rebuke was added that of the Lord: because of her pride and arrogance, Michal "had no child unto the day of her death."

The solemn ceremonies attending the removal of the ark had made a lasting impression upon the people of Israel, arousing a deeper interest in the sanctuary service and kindling anew their zeal for Jehovah. David endeavored by every means in his power to deepen these impressions. The service of song was made a regular part of religious worship, and David composed psalms, not only for the use of the priests in the sanctuary service, but also to be sung by the people in their journeys to the national altar at the annual feasts. The influence thus exerted was far-reaching, and it resulted in freeing the nation from idolatry. Many of the surrounding peoples, beholding the prosperity of Israel, were led to think favorably of Israel's God, who had done such great things for His people. *Patriarchs and Prophets,* 711.

David Plans to Build a Temple

The tabernacle built by Moses, with all that appertained to the sanctuary service, except the ark, was still at Gibeah. It was David's purpose to make Jerusalem the religious center of the nation. He had erected a palace for himself, and he felt that it was not fitting for the ark of God to rest within a tent. He determined to build for it a temple of such magnificence as should express Israel's appreciation of the honor granted the nation in the abiding presence of Jehovah their King. Communicating his purpose to the prophet Nathan, he received the encouraging response, "Do all that is in thine heart; for the Lord is with thee."

But that same night the word of the Lord came to Nathan, giving him a message for the king. David was to be deprived of the privilege of building a house for God, but he was granted an assurance of the divine favor to him, to his posterity, and to the kingdom of Israel: "Thus saith Jehovah of hosts; I took thee from the sheepcote, from following the sheep, to be ruler over

My people, over Israel; and I was with thee whithersoever thou wentest, and have cut off all thine enemies out of thy sight, and have made thee a great name, like unto the name of the great men that are in the earth. Moreover I will appoint a place for My people Israel, and will plant them, that they may dwell in a place of their own, and move no more; neither shall the children of wickedness afflict them any more, as beforetime."

As David had desired to build a house for God, the promise was given. "The Lord telleth thee that He will make thee a house ... I will set up thy seed after thee. He shall build a house for My name, and I will stablish the throne of his kingdom forever."

The reason why David was not to build the temple was declared: "Thou hast shed blood abundantly, and hast made great wars: thou shalt not build a house unto My name. Behold, a son shall be born to thee, who shall be a man of rest; and I will give him rest from all his enemies: his name shall be Solomon [peaceable], and I will give peace and quietness unto Israel in his days. He shall build a house for My name." 1 Chronicles 22:8–10.

Though the cherished purpose of his heart had been denied, David received the message with gratitude. "Who am I, O Lord God?" he exclaimed, "and what is my house, that Thou hast brought me hitherto? And this was yet a small thing in Thy sight, O Lord God; but Thou hast spoken also of Thy servant's house for a great while to come;" and he then renewed his covenant with God.

David knew that it would be an honor to his name and would bring glory to his government to perform the work that he had purposed in his heart to do, but he was ready to submit his will to the will of God. The grateful resignation thus manifested is rarely seen, even among Christians. How often do those who have passed the strength of manhood cling to the hope of accomplishing some great work upon which their hearts are set, but which they are unfitted to perform! God's providence may speak to them, as did His prophet to David, declaring that the work which they so much desire is not committed to them. It is theirs to prepare the way for another to accomplish it. But instead of gratefully submitting to the divine direction, many fall back as if slighted and rejected, feeling that if they cannot do the one thing which they desire to do, they will do nothing. Many cling with desperate energy to responsibilities which they are incapable of bearing, and vainly endeavor to accomplish a work for which they are insufficient, while that which they might do, lies neglected. And because of this lack of co-operation on their part the greater work is hindered or frustrated.

David, in his covenant with Jonathan, had promised that when he should have rest from his enemies he would show kindness to the house of Saul. In his prosperity, mindful of this covenant, the king made inquiry, "Is there yet any that is left of the house of Saul, that I may show him kindness for Jonathan's sake?" He was told of a son of Jonathan, Mephibosheth, who had been lame from childhood. At the time of Saul's defeat by the Philistines at Jezreel, the nurse of this child, attempting to flee with him, had let him fall, thus making him a lifelong cripple. David now summoned the young man to court and received him with great kindness. The private possessions of Saul were restored to him for the support of his household; but the son of Jonathan was himself to be the constant guest of the king, sitting daily at the royal table. Through reports from the enemies of David, Mephibosheth had been led to cherish a strong prejudice against him as a usurper; but the monarch's generous and courteous reception of him and his continued kindness won the heart of the young man; he became strongly attached to David, and, like his father Jonathan, he felt that his interest was one with that of the king whom God had chosen. *Patriarchs and Prophets*, 711–713.

War Again with the Philistines and Ammonites

After David's establishment upon the throne of Israel the nation enjoyed a long interval of peace. The surrounding peoples, seeing the strength and unity of the kingdom, soon thought it prudent to desist from open hostilities; and David, occupied with the organization and upbuilding of his kingdom, refrained from aggressive war. At last, however, he made war upon Israel's old enemies, the Philistines, and upon the Moabites, and succeeded in overcoming both and making them tributary.

Then there was formed against the kingdom of David a vast coalition of the surrounding nations, out of which grew the greatest wars and victories of his reign and the most extensive accessions to his power. This hostile alliance, which really sprang from jealousy of David's increasing power, had been wholly unprovoked by him. The circumstances that led to its rise were these:

Tidings were received at Jerusalem announcing the death of Nahash, king of the Ammonites—a monarch who had shown kindness to David when he was a fugitive from the rage of Saul. Now, desiring to express his grateful appreciation of the favor shown him in his distress, David sent ambassadors with a message of sympathy to Hanun, the son and successor of the Ammonite king. "Said David, I will show kindness unto Hanun the son of Nahash, as his father showed kindness unto me."

But his courteous act was misinterpreted. They could have no conception of the generous spirit that had inspired David's message. When Satan controls the minds of men he will excite envy and suspicion which will misconstrue the very best intentions. Listening to his counselors, Hanun regarded David's messengers as spies, and loaded them with scorn and insult.

The Ammonites had been permitted to carry out the evil purposes of their hearts without restraint, that their real character might be revealed to David. It was not God's will that Israel should enter into a league with this treacherous heathen people.

The Hebrews did not wait for the invasion of their country. Their forces, under Joab, crossed the Jordan and advanced toward the Ammonite capital. As the Hebrew captain led his army to the field he sought to inspire them for the conflict, saying, "Be of good courage, and let us behave ourselves valiantly for our people, and for the cities of our God: and let the Lord do that which is good in His sight." 1 Chronicles 19:13. The united forces of the allies were overcome in the first engagement. But they were not yet willing to give over the contest, and the next year renewed the war. The king of Syria gathered his forces, threatening Israel with an immense army. David, realizing how much dependent upon the result of this contest, took the field in person, and by the blessing of God inflicted upon the allies a defeat so disastrous that the Syrians, from Lebanon to the Euphrates, not only gave up the war, but became tributary to Israel. Against the Ammonites David pushed the war with vigor, until their strongholds fell and the whole region came under the dominion of Israel. *Patriarchs and Prophets,* 713–715.

Chapter Five

David's Moral Fall

His religious character was sincere and fervent. It was while David was thus true to God, and possessing these exalted traits of character, that God calls him a man after his own heart. When exalted to the throne, his general course was in striking contrast with the kings of other nations. He abhorred idolatry, and zealously kept the people of Israel from being seduced into idolatry by the surrounding nations. He was greatly beloved and honored by his people.

He often conquered, and triumphed. He increased in wealth and greatness. But his prosperity had an influence to lead him from God. His temptations were many and strong. He finally fell into the common practice of other kings around him, of having a plurality of wives, and his life was imbittered by the evil results of polygamy. His first wrong was in taking more than one wife, thus departing from God's wise arrangement. This departure from right, prepared the way for greater errors. The kingly idolatrous nations considered it an addition to their honor and dignity to have many wives, and David regarded it an honor to his throne to possess several wives. But he was made to see the wretched evil of such a course by the unhappy discord, rivalry and jealousy among his numerous wives and children. *Spiritual Gifts,* vol. 4, 86.

It was the spirit of self-confidence and self-exaltation that prepared the way for David's fall. Flattery and the subtle allurements of power and luxury were not without effect upon him.

Intercourse with surrounding nations also exerted an influence for evil. According to the customs prevailing among Eastern rulers, crimes not to be tolerated in subjects were uncondemned in the king; the monarch was not under obligation to exercise the same self-restraint as the subject. All this tended to lessen David's sense of the exceeding sinfulness of sin. And instead of relying in humility upon the power of Jehovah, he began to trust to his own wisdom and might. As soon as Satan can separate the soul from God, the only Source of strength, he will seek to arouse the unholy desires of man's carnal nature. The work of the enemy is not abrupt; it is not, at the outset, sudden and startling; it is a secret undermining of the strongholds of principle. It begins in apparently small things—the neglect to be true to God and to rely upon Him wholly, the disposition to follow the customs and practices of the world.

> *It was the spirit of self-confidence and self-exaltation that prepared the way for David's fall*

Before the conclusion of the war with the Ammonites, David, leaving the conduct of the army to Joab, returned to Jerusalem. The Syrians had already submitted to Israel, and the complete overthrow of the Ammonites appeared certain. David was surrounded by the fruits of victory and the honors of his wise and able rule. It was now, while he was at ease and unguarded, that the tempter seized the opportunity to occupy his mind. The fact that God had taken David into so close connection with Himself and had manifested so great favor toward him, should have been to him the strongest of incentives to preserve his character unblemished. But when in ease and self-security he let go his hold upon God, David yielded to Satan and brought upon his soul the stain of guilt. He, the Heaven-appointed leader of the nation, chosen by God to execute His law, himself trampled upon its precepts. He who should have been a terror to evildoers, by his own act strengthened their hands.

Amid the perils of his earlier life David in conscious integrity could trust his case with God. The Lord's hand had guided him safely past the unnumbered snares that had been laid for his feet. But now, guilty and unrepentant, he did not ask help and guidance from Heaven, but sought to extricate himself from the dangers in which sin had involved him. Bathsheba, whose fatal beauty had proved a snare to the king, was the wife of Uriah the Hittite, one of David's bravest and most faithful officers. None could foresee what would be the result should the crime become known. The law of God pronounced the adulterer guilty of death, and the proud-spirited soldier, so shamefully wronged, might avenge himself by taking the life of the king or by exciting the nation to revolt. *Patriarchs and Prophets,* 718.

Had King David been engaged in some useful employment, he would not have been guilty of the murder of Uriah. Satan is ever ready to employ him who does not employ himself. The mind which is continually striving to rise to the height of intellectual greatness will find no time for cheap, foolish thoughts, which are the parent of evil actions. *Gospel Workers* (1892), 168.

David Plans Uriah's Murder

Every effort which David made to conceal his guilt proved unavailing. He had betrayed himself into the power of Satan; danger surrounded him, dishonor more bitter than death was before him. There appeared but one way of escape, and in his desperation he was hurried on to add murder to adultery. He who had compassed the destruction of Saul was seeking to lead David also to ruin. Though the temptations were different, they were alike in leading to transgression of God's law. David reasoned that if Uriah were slain by the hand of enemies in battle, the guilt of his death could not be traced home to the king, Bathsheba would be free to become David's wife, suspicion could be averted, and the royal honor would be maintained.

Uriah was made the bearer of his own death warrant. A letter sent by his hand to Joab from the king commanded, "Set ye Uriah in the forefront of the hottest battle, and retire ye from him, that he may be smitten, and die." Joab, already stained with the guilt of one wanton murder, did not hesitate to obey the king's instructions, and Uriah fell by the sword of the children of Ammon. *Patriarchs and Prophets*, 718, 719.

His crime in the case of Uriah and Bathsheba, was heinous in the sight of God. A just and impartial God did not sanction or excuse these sins in David, but sent a reproof and heavy denunciation by Nathan, his prophet, which portrayed in living colors his grievous offense. David had been blinded to his wonderful departure from God. He had excused his own sinful course to himself, until his ways seemed passable in his own eyes. One wrong step had prepared the way for another, until his sins called for the rebuke from Jehovah through Nathan. David awakens as from a dream. He feels the sense of his sin. He does not seek to excuse his course, or palliate his sin, as did Saul; but with remorse and sincere grief, he bows his head before the prophet of God, and acknowledges his guilt. Nathan tells David that, because of his repentance and humble confession, God will forgive his sin, and avert a part of the threatened calamity, and spare his life; yet he should be punished, because he had given great occasion to the enemies of the Lord to blaspheme. This occasion has been improved by the enemies of God, from David's day until the present time. Skeptics have assailed Christianity, and ridiculed the Bible, because David gave them occasion. They bring up to Christians the case of David, his sin in the case of Uriah and Bathsheba, his polygamy, and then assert that David is called a man after God's own heart, and that if the Bible record is correct, God justified David in his crimes.

I was shown that it was when David was pure, and walking in the counsel of God, that God called him a man after his own heart. When David departed from God, and stained his virtuous character by his crimes, he was no longer a man after God's own heart. God did not in the least degree justify him in his sins, but sent Nathan, his prophet, with dreadful denunciations to David because he had transgressed the commandment of the Lord. God shows his displeasure at David's having a plurality of wives, by visiting him with judgments, and permitting evils to rise up against him from his own house. The terrible calamity that God permitted to come upon David, who, for his integrity, was once called a man after God's own heart, is evidence to after generations that God would not justify any one in transgressing his commandments; but that he would surely punish the guilty, however righteous and favored of God they might once have been while they followed the Lord in purity of heart. When the righteous turn from their righteousness and do evil, their past righteousness will not save them from the wrath of a just and holy God. *Spirit of Prophecy,* vol. 1, 379.

Bathsheba observed the customary days of mourning for her husband; and at their close "David sent and fetched her to his house, and she became his wife." He whose tender conscience and high sense of honor would not permit him, even when in peril of his life, to put forth his hand against the Lord's anointed, had so fallen that he could wrong and murder one of his most faithful and most valiant soldiers, and hope to enjoy undisturbed the reward of his sin. Alas! how had the fine gold become dim! how had the most fine gold changed! ... For the sake of Israel also there was a necessity for God to interpose. As time passed on, David's sin toward Bathsheba became known, and suspicion was excited that he had planned the death of Uriah. The Lord was dishonored. He had favored and exalted David, and David's sin misrepresented the character of God and cast reproach upon His name. It tended to lower the standard of godliness in Israel, to lessen in many minds the abhorrence of sin; while those who did not love and fear God were by it emboldened in transgression. *Patriarchs and Prophets,* 720.

Nathan Rebukes David

Nathan the prophet was bidden to bear a message of reproof to David. It was a message terrible in its severity. To few sovereigns could such a reproof be given but at the price of certain death to the reprover. Nathan delivered the divine sentence unflinchingly, yet with such heaven-born wisdom as to engage the sympathies of the king, to arouse his conscience, and to call from his lips the sentence of death upon himself. Appealing to David as the divinely appointed guardian of his people's rights, the prophet repeated a story of wrong and oppression that demanded redress.

"There were two men in one city," he said, "the one rich, and the other poor. The rich man had exceeding many flocks and herds: but the poor man had nothing, save one little ewe lamb, which he had bought and nourished up: and it grew up together with him, and with his children; it did eat of his own meat, and drank of his own cup, and lay in his bosom, and was unto him as a daughter. And there came a traveler unto the rich man, and he spared to take of his own flock and of his own herd, to dress for the wayfaring man that was come unto him; but took the poor man's lamb, and dressed it for the man that was come to him."

The anger of the king was roused, and he exclaimed, "As the Lord liveth, the man that hath done this thing is worthy to die. And he shall restore the lamb fourfold, because he did this thing, and because he had no pity." 2 Samuel 12:5, 6, margin.

Nathan fixed his eyes upon the king; then, lifting his right hand to heaven, he solemnly declared, "Thou art the man." "Wherefore," he continued, "hast thou despised the commandment of the Lord, to do evil in His sight?" The guilty may attempt, as David had done, to conceal their crime from men; they may seek to bury the evil deed forever from human sight or knowledge; but "all things are naked and opened unto the eyes of Him with whom we have to do." Hebrews 4:13. "There is nothing covered, that shall not be revealed; and hid, that shall not be known." Matthew 10:26.

Nathan declared: "Thus saith the Lord God of Israel, I anointed thee king over Israel, and I delivered thee out of the hand of Saul.

... Wherefore hast thou despised the commandment of the Lord, to do evil in His sight? thou hast killed Uriah the Hittite with the sword, and hast taken his wife to be thy wife, and hast slain him with the sword of the children of Ammon. Now therefore the sword shall never depart from thine house. Behold, I will raise up evil against thee out of thine own house, and I will take thy wives before thine eyes, and give them unto thy neighbor. For thou didst it secretly; but I will do this thing before all Israel, and before the sun." The prophet's rebuke touched the heart of David; conscience was aroused; his guilt appeared in all its enormity. His soul was bowed in penitence before God. With trembling lips he said, "I have sinned against the Lord." All wrong done to others reaches back from the injured one to God. David had committed a grievous sin, toward both Uriah and Bathsheba, and he keenly felt this. But infinitely greater was his sin against God. *Patriarchs and Prophets,* 720–722.

> *All wrong done to others reaches back from the injured one to God*

When David sinned against Uriah and his wife, he pleaded before God for forgiveness. He declares: "Against Thee, Thee only, have I sinned, and done this evil in Thy sight." All wrong done to others reaches back from the injured one to God. Therefore David seeks for pardon, not from a priest, but from the Creator of man. He prays: "Have mercy upon me, O God, according to Thy lovingkindness: according unto the multitude of Thy tender mercies blot out my transgressions." *Testimonies for the Church,* vol. 5, 639.

David's repentance was sincere and deep. There was no effort to palliate his crime. No desire to escape the judgments threatened, inspired his prayer. But he saw the enormity of his transgression against God; he saw the defilement of his soul; he loathed his sin. It was not for pardon only that he prayed, but for purity of heart. David did not in despair give over the struggle. In the promises of God to repentant sinners he saw the evidence of his pardon and acceptance.

> "For Thou desirest not sacrifice; else would I give it: Thou delightest not in burnt offering.
>
> The sacrifices of God are a broken spirit:
>
> A broken and a contrite heart, O God, Thou wilt not despise." Psalm 51:16, 17. ...

This passage in David's history is full of significance to the repenting sinner. It is one of the most forcible illustrations given us of the struggles and temptations of humanity, and of genuine repentance toward God and faith in our Lord Jesus Christ. Through all the ages it has proved a source of encouragement to souls that, having fallen into sin, were struggling under the burden of their guilt. Thousands of the children of God, who have been betrayed into sin, when ready to give up to despair have remembered how David's sincere repentance and confession were accepted by God, notwithstanding he suffered for his transgression; and they also have taken courage to repent and try again to walk in the way of God's commandments. *Patriarchs and Prophets,* 725, 726.

We need just such lessons as the Bible gives. The sorrow and penitence of the guilty and the wailings of the sin-sick soul, come to us from the past, telling that man was then, as now, in need of the pardoning mercy of God. The record shows us that while he is a punisher of crime, he pities and forgives the repenting sinner. In his good providence the Lord has seen fit to teach and warn his people in this way through the Sacred Writings, that all might understand his will. If God's people would recognize his dealings with them, and accept his teachings, they would find a straight path for their feet, and a light to guide them through darkness and discouragement. David learned wisdom from God's dealings with him, and bowed in humility beneath the chastisement of the Most High. The faithful portrayal of his true state by the prophet Nathan, made David acquainted with his own sins and aided him to put them away. He accepted counsel meekly, and humbled himself before God. "The law of the Lord," he exclaims, "is perfect, converting the soul." *Review and Herald*, January 22, 1880.

Consequences of Sin

David was made to feel bitterly the fruits of wrong-doing. His sons acted over the sins of which he had been guilty. Amnon committed a great crime; Absalom revenged it by slaying him. Thus was David's sin brought continually to his mind, and he made to feel the full weight of the injustice done to Uriah and Bathsheba.

Absalom, his own son, whom he loved above all his children, rebelled against him. By his remarkable beauty, winning manners, and pretended kindness, he cunningly stole the hearts of the people. He did not possess benevolence at heart, but was ambitious, and, as his course shows, would resort to intrigue and crime to obtain the kingdom. He would have requited his father's love and kindness by taking his life. He was proclaimed king by his followers in Hebron, and led them out to pursue his father. He was defeated and slain.

David was brought into great distress by this rebellion. It was unlike any war that he had been connected with. His wisdom from God, with his energy and warlike skill, had enabled him to successfully resist the assaults of his enemies. But this unnatural warfare, arising in his own house, and the rebel being his own son, seemed to confuse and weaken his calm judgment. And the knowledge that this evil had been predicted by the prophet, and that he had brought it upon himself by transgressing the commandments of God, destroyed his skill and former unequaled courage. *Spirit of Prophecy,* vol. 1, 382.

The evil results of David's unjust indulgence toward Amnon were not ended, for it was here that Absalom's alienation from his father began. After he fled to Geshur, David, feeling that the crime of his son demanded some punishment, refused him permission to return. And this had a tendency to increase rather than to lessen the inextricable evils in which the king had come to be involved. Absalom, energetic, ambitious, and unprincipled, shut out by his exile from participation in the affairs of the kingdom, soon gave himself up to dangerous scheming.

At the close of two years Joab determined to effect a reconciliation between the father and his son. And with this object in view he secured the services of a woman of Tekoah, reputed for wisdom. Instructed by Joab, the woman represented herself to David as a widow whose two sons had been her only comfort and support. In a quarrel one of these had slain the other, and now all the relatives of the family demanded that the survivor should be given up to the avenger of blood. "And so," said the mother, "they shall quench my coal which is left, and shall not leave to my husband neither name nor remainder upon the earth." The king's feelings were touched by this appeal, and he assured the woman of the royal protection for her son.

After drawing from him repeated promises for the young man's safety, she entreated the king's forbearance, declaring that he had spoken as one at fault, in that he did not fetch home again his banished. "For," she said, "we must needs die, and are as water spilt on the ground, which cannot be gathered up again; neither doth God respect any person; yet doth He devise means, that His banished be not expelled from Him." This tender and touching portrayal of the love of God toward the sinner—coming as it did from Joab, the rude soldier—is a striking evidence of the familiarity of the Israelites with the great truths of redemption.

David's Moral Fall | 91

The king, feeling his own need of God's mercy, could not resist this appeal. To Joab the command was given, "Go therefore, bring the young man Absalom again."

Absalom was permitted to return to Jerusalem, but not to appear at court or to meet his father. David had begun to see the evil effects of his indulgence toward his children; and tenderly as he loved this beautiful and gifted son, he felt it necessary, as a lesson both to Absalom and to the people, that abhorrence for such a crime should be manifested. Absalom lived two years in his own house, but banished from the court. His sister dwelt with him, and her presence kept alive the memory of the irreparable wrong she had suffered. In the popular estimation the prince was a hero rather than an offender. And having this advantage, he set himself to gain the hearts of the people. His personal appearance was such as to win the admiration of all beholders. "In all Israel there was none to be so much praised as Absalom for his beauty: from the sole of his foot even to the crown of his head there was no blemish in him." It was not wise for the king to leave a man of Absalom's character—ambitious, impulsive, and passionate—to brood for two years over supposed grievances. And David's action in permitting him to return to Jerusalem, and yet refusing to admit him to his presence, enlisted in his behalf the sympathies of the people.

With the memory ever before him of his own transgression of the law of God, David seemed morally paralyzed; he was weak and irresolute, when before his sin he had been courageous and decided. His influence with the people had been weakened. And all this favored the designs of his unnatural son. *Patriarchs and Prophets,* 728, 729.

Chapter Six

Absalom's Rebellion

Absalom set forth for Hebron, and there went with him "two hundred men out of Jerusalem, that were called; and they went in their simplicity, and they knew not anything." These men went with Absalom, little thinking that their love for the son was leading them into rebellion against the father. Upon arriving at Hebron, Absalom immediately summoned Ahithophel, one of the chief counselors of David, a man in high repute for wisdom, whose opinion was thought to be as safe and wise as that of an oracle. Ahithophel joined the conspirators, and his support made the cause of Absalom appear certain of success, attracting to his standard many influential men from all parts of the land. As the trumpet of revolt was sounded, the prince's spies throughout the country spread the tidings that Absalom was king, and many of the people gathered to him.

Meanwhile the alarm was carried to Jerusalem, to the king. David was suddenly aroused, to see rebellion breaking out close beside his throne. His own son—the son whom he had loved and trusted—had been planning to seize his crown and doubtless to take his life. In his great peril David shook off the depression that had so long rested upon him, and with the spirit of his earlier years he prepared to meet this terrible emergency. Absalom was mustering his forces at Hebron, only twenty miles away. The rebels would soon be at the gates of Jerusalem.

From his palace David looked out upon his capital—"beautiful for situation, the joy of the whole earth, ... the city of the great King." Psalm 48:2. He shuddered at the thought of exposing it to carnage and devastation. Should he call to his help the subjects still loyal to his throne, and make a stand to hold his capital? Should he permit Jerusalem to be deluged with blood? His decision was taken. The horrors of war should not fall upon the chosen city. He would leave Jerusalem, and then test the fidelity of his people, giving them an opportunity to rally to his support. In this great crisis it was his duty to God and to his people to maintain the authority with which Heaven had invested him. The issue of the conflict he would trust with God.

Sorrowful Exodus from Jerusalem

In humility and sorrow David passed out of the gate of Jerusalem—driven from his throne, from his palace, from the ark of God, by the insurrection of his cherished son. The people followed in long, sad procession, like a funeral train. David's bodyguard of Cherethites, Pelethites, and six hundred Gittites from Gath, under the command of Ittai, accompanied the king. But David, with characteristic unselfishness, could not consent that these strangers who had sought his protection should be involved in his calamity. He expressed surprise that they should be ready to make this sacrifice for him. Then said the king to Ittai the Gittite, "Wherefore goest thou also with us? return to thy place, and abide with the king: for thou art a stranger, and also an exile. Whereas thou camest but yesterday, should I this day make thee go up and down with us? seeing I go whither I may, return thou, and take back thy brethren: mercy and truth be with thee."

Ittai answered, "As the Lord liveth, and as my lord the king liveth, surely in what place my lord the king shall be, whether in death or life, even there also will thy servant be." These men had been converted from paganism to the worship of Jehovah, and nobly they now proved their fidelity to their God and their king. David, with grateful heart, accepted their devotion to his apparently sinking cause, and all passed over the brook Kidron on the way toward the wilderness.

Again the procession halted. A company clad in holy vestments was approaching. "And lo Zadok also, and all the Levites were with him, bearing the ark of the covenant of God." The followers of David looked upon this as a happy omen. The presence of that sacred symbol was to them a pledge of their deliverance and ultimate victory. It would inspire the people with courage to rally to the king. Its absence from Jerusalem would bring terror to the adherents of Absalom.

At sight of the ark joy and hope for a brief moment thrilled the heart of David. But soon other thoughts came to him. As the appointed ruler of God's heritage he was under solemn responsibility. Not personal interests, but the glory of God and the good of his people, were to be uppermost in the mind of Israel's king. God, who dwelt between the cherubim, had said of Jerusalem, "This is My rest" (Psalm 132:14); and without divine authority neither priest nor king had a right to remove therefrom the symbol of His presence. And David knew that his heart and life must be in harmony with the divine precepts, else the ark would be the means of disaster rather than of success. His great sin was ever before him. He recognized in this conspiracy the just judgment of God. The sword that was not to depart from his house had been unsheathed. He knew not what the result of the struggle might be. It was not for him to remove from the capital of the nation the sacred statutes which embodied the will of their divine Sovereign, which were the constitution of the realm and the foundation of its prosperity.

He commanded Zadok, "Carry back the ark of God into the city: if I shall find favor in the eyes of the Lord, He will bring me again, and show me both it and His habitation: but if He thus say, I have no delight in thee; behold, here am I, let Him do to me as seemeth good unto Him."

David added, "Art not thou a seer?" —a man appointed of God to instruct the people. "Return into the city in peace, and your two sons with you, Ahimaaz thy son, and Jonathan the son of Abiathar. See, I will tarry in the plain of the wilderness, until there come word from you to certify me." In the city the priests might do him good service by learning the movements and purposes of the rebels, and secretly communicating them to the king by their sons, Ahimaaz and Jonathan.

Ahithophel Joins Absalom

As the priests turned back toward Jerusalem a deeper shadow fell upon the departing throng. Their king a fugitive, themselves outcasts, forsaken even by the ark of God—the future was dark with terror and foreboding. "And David went up by the ascent of Mount Olivet, and wept as he went up, and had his head covered, and he went barefoot: and all the people that was with him covered every man his head, and they went up, weeping as they went up. And one told David, saying, Ahithophel is among the conspirators with Absalom." Again David was forced to recognize in his calamities the results of his own sin. The defection of Ahithophel, the ablest and most wily of political leaders, was prompted by revenge for the family disgrace involved in the wrong to Bathsheba, who was his granddaughter. *Patriarchs and Prophets,* 730–735.

David was never more worthy of admiration than in his hour of adversity. Never was this cedar of God truly greater than when wrestling with the storm and tempest. He was a man of the keenest temperament, which might have been raised to the strongest feelings of resentment. He was cut to the quick with the imputation of unmerited wrong. Reproach, he tells us, had broken his heart. And it would not have been surprising if, stung to madness, he had given vent to his feelings of uncontrollable irritation, to bursts of vehement rage, and expressions of revenge. But there was nothing of this which would naturally be expected of a man with his stamp of character. With spirits broken and in tearful emotion, but without one expression of repining, he turns his back upon the scenes of his glory and also of his crime, and pursues his flight for his life. *SDA Bible Commentaries*, vol. 3, 1146.

"And David said, O Lord, I pray Thee, turn the counsel of Ahithophel into foolishness." Upon reaching the top of the mount, the king bowed in prayer, casting upon God the burden of his soul and humbly supplicating divine mercy. His prayer seemed to be at once answered. Hushai the Archite, a wise and able counselor, who had proved himself a faithful friend to David, now came to him with his robes rent and with earth upon his head, to cast in his fortunes with the dethroned and fugitive king. David saw, as by a divine enlightenment, that this man, faithful and truehearted, was the one needed to serve the interests of the king in the councils at the capital. At David's request Hushai returned to Jerusalem to offer his services to Absalom and defeat the crafty counsel of Ahithophel. *Patriarchs and Prophets,* 735.

Shimei, a kinsman of Saul, who had ever been envious of David because he received the throne and kingly honors which had once been given to Saul, improved this opportunity of venting his rebellious rage upon David in his misfortune. He cursed the king, and cast stones and dirt at him and his servants, and accused David of being a bloody and mischievous man. The followers of David beg permission to go and take his life; but David rebukes them, and tells them to "let him curse, because the Lord hath said unto him, Curse David. Who shall then say, Wherefore hast thou done so?" Behold my son "seeketh my life; how much more now may this Benjamite do it? Let him alone, and let him curse; for the Lord hath bidden him."

David's Remorse and Humility

He thus acknowledges, before his people and chief men, that this is the punishment God has brought upon him because of his sin, which has given the enemies of the Lord occasion to blaspheme; that the enraged Benjamite might be accomplishing his part of the punishment predicted, and that if he bore these things with humility, the Lord would lessen his affliction, and turn the curse of Shimei into a blessing. David does not manifest the spirit of an unconverted man. He shows that he has had an experience in the things of God. He manifests a disposition to receive correction from God, and, in confidence turns to him as his only trust. God rewards David's humble trust in him, by defeating the counsel of Ahithophel, and preserving his life. *Spirit of Prophecy,* vol. 1, 382, 383.

Conscience was uttering bitter and humiliating truths to David. While his faithful subjects wondered at his sudden reverse of fortune, it was no mystery to the king. He had often had forebodings of an hour like this. He had wondered that God had so long borne with his sins, and had delayed the merited retribution. And now in his hurried and sorrowful flight, his feet bare, his royal robes changed for sackcloth, the lamentations of his followers awaking the echoes of the hills, he thought of his loved capital—of the place which had been the scene of his sin—and as he remembered the goodness and long-suffering of God, he was not altogether without hope. He felt that the Lord would still deal with him in mercy. *Patriarchs and Prophets,* 737.

Never was David dearer to the heart of infinite love than when, conscious [conscience] smitten, he fled for his life from his enemies, who were stirred into rebellion by his own son. In tearful, heartbroken utterances, he presented his case to God, and pursued his sorrowful course; but no word of repining escaped from his lips. The Lord says, "As many as I love, I rebuke and chasten; be zealous therefore, and repent." There is a blessing pronounced upon all who mourn. Had there been no mourners in our world, Christ could not have revealed to man the parental character of God. Those oppressed by the conviction of sin are to know the blessedness of forgiveness, and to have their transgressions blotted out. Had there been none who mourn, the sufficiency of Christ's expiation for sin would not have been understood. *Signs of the Times*, August 8, 1895.

Many a wrongdoer has excused his own sin by pointing to David's fall, but how few there are who manifest David's penitence and humility. How few would bear reproof and retribution with the patience and fortitude that he manifested. He had confessed his sin, and for years had sought to do his duty as a faithful servant of God; he had labored for the upbuilding of his kingdom, and under his rule it had attained to strength and prosperity never reached before. He had gathered rich stores of material for the building of the house of God, and now was all the labor of his life to be swept away? Must the results of years of consecrated toil, the work of genius and devotion and statesmanship, pass into the hands of his reckless and traitorous son, who regarded not the honor of God nor the prosperity of Israel? How natural it would have seemed for David to murmur against God in this great affliction!

But he saw in his own sin the cause of his trouble. The words of the prophet Micah breathe the spirit that inspired David's heart. "When I sit in darkness, the Lord shall be a light unto me. I will bear the indignation of the Lord, because I have sinned against Him, until He plead my cause, and execute judgment for me." Micah 7:8, 9. And the Lord did not forsake David. This chapter in his experience, when, under cruelest wrong and insult, he shows himself to be humble, unselfish, generous, and submissive, is one of the noblest in his whole experience. Never was the ruler of

Israel more truly great in the sight of heaven than at this hour of his deepest outward humiliation.

Had God permitted David to go on unrebuked in sin, and while transgressing the divine precepts, to remain in peace and prosperity upon his throne, the skeptic and infidel might have had some excuse for citing the history of David as a reproach to the religion of the Bible. But in the experience through which He caused David to pass, the Lord shows that He cannot tolerate or excuse sin. And David's history enables us to see also the great ends which God has in view in His dealings with sin; it enables us to trace, even through darkest judgments, the working out of His purposes of mercy and beneficence. He caused David to pass under the rod, but He did not destroy him; the furnace is to purify, but not to consume. The Lord says, "If they break My statutes, and keep not My commandments; then will I visit their transgression with the rod, and their iniquity with stripes. Nevertheless My loving-kindness will I not utterly take from him, nor suffer My faithfulness to fail." Psalm 89:31–33.

Absalom Possesses Jerusalem

Soon after David left Jerusalem, Absalom and his army entered, and without a struggle took possession of the stronghold of Israel. Hushai was among the first to greet the new-crowned monarch, and the prince was surprised and gratified at the accession of his father's old friend and counselor. Absalom was confident of success. Thus far his schemes had prospered, and eager to strengthen his throne and secure the confidence of the nation, he welcomed Hushai to his court.

Absalom was now surrounded by a large force, but it was mostly composed of men untrained for war. As yet they had not been brought into conflict. Ahithophel well knew that David's situation was far from hopeless. A large part of the nation were still true to him; he was surrounded by tried warriors, who were faithful to their king, and his army was commanded by able and experienced generals. Ahithophel knew that after the first burst of enthusiasm in favor of the new king, a reaction would come. Should the rebellion fail, Absalom might be able to secure a reconciliation with his father; then Ahithophel, as his chief counselor, would be held most guilty for the rebellion; upon him the heaviest punishment would fall. To prevent Absalom from retracing his steps, Ahithophel counseled him to an act that in the eyes of the whole nation would make reconciliation impossible. With hellish cunning this wily and unprincipled statesman urged Absalom to add the crime of incest to that of rebellion. In the sight of all Israel he was to take to himself his father's concubines, according to the custom of oriental nations, thus declaring that he succeeded to his father's throne. And Absalom carried out the vile suggestion. Thus was fulfilled the word of God to David by the prophet, "Behold, I will raise up evil against thee out of thine own house, and I will take thy wives before thine eyes, and give them unto thy neighbor For thou didst it secretly: but I will do this thing before all Israel, and before the sun." 2 Samuel 12:11,12. Not that God prompted these acts of wickedness, but because of David's sin He did not exercise His power to prevent them. *Patriarchs and Prophets,* 737, 738.

Ahithophel's Demise

Ahithophel urged upon Absalom the necessity of immediate action against David. This plan was approved by the king's counselors. Had it been followed, David would surely have been slain, unless the Lord had directly interposed to save him. But a wisdom higher than that of the renowned Ahithophel was directing events. ... Hushai had not been called to the council, and he would not intrude himself unasked, lest suspicion should be drawn upon him as a spy; but after the assembly had dispersed, Absalom, who had a high regard for the judgment of his father's counselor, submitted to him the plan of Ahithophel. Hushai saw that if the proposed plan were followed, David would be lost. And he said, "The counsel that Ahithophel hath given is not good at this time." ... He suggested a plan attractive to a vain and selfish nature, fond of the show of power "And Absalom and all the men of Israel said, The counsel of Hushai the Archite is better than the counsel of Ahithophel." But there was one who was not deceived—one who clearly foresaw the result of this fatal mistake of Absalom's.

> *This plan was approved by the king's counselors. Had it been followed, David would surely have been slain, unless the Lord had directly interposed to save him*

Ahithophel knew that the cause of the rebels was lost. And he knew that whatever might be the fate of the prince, there was no hope for the counselor who had instigated his greatest crimes. Ahithophel had encouraged Absalom in rebellion; he had counseled him to the most abominable wickedness, to the dishonor of his father; he had advised the slaying of David and had planned its accomplishment; he had cut off the last possibility of his own reconciliation with the king; and now another was preferred before him, even by Absalom.

Jealous, angry, and desperate, Ahithophel "gat him home to his house, to his city, and put his household in order, and hanged himself, and died." Such was the result of the wisdom of one, who, with all his high endowments, did not make God his counselor. *Conflict and Courage,* 183.

David Escapes Beyond Jordan

Hushai, not certain that his counsel would be followed by the fickle king, lost no time in warning David to escape beyond Jordan without delay. To the priests, who were to forward it by their sons, Hushai sent the message: "Thus and thus did Ahithophel counsel Absalom and the elders of Israel; and thus and thus have I counseled. Now therefore ... lodge not this night in the plains of the wilderness, but speedily pass over; lest the king be swallowed up, and all the people that are with him."

The young men were suspected and pursued, yet they succeeded in performing their perilous mission. David, spent with toil and grief after that first day of flight, received the message that he must cross the Jordan that night, for his son was seeking his life.

What were the feelings of the father and king, so cruelly wronged, in this terrible peril? "A mighty valiant man," a man of war, a king, whose word was law, betrayed by his son whom he had loved and indulged and unwisely trusted, wronged and deserted by subjects bound to him by the strongest ties of honor and fealty—in what words did David pour out the feelings of his soul? In the hour of his darkest trial David's heart was stayed upon God, and he sang:

"Lord, how are they increased that trouble me! Many are they that rise up against me.

Many there be which say of my soul, There is no help for him in God.

But Thou, O Lord, art a shield for me; My glory, and the lifter up of mine head. I cried unto the Lord with my voice, And He heard me out of His holy hill.

I laid me down and slept;

I awaked; for the Lord sustained me.

I will not be afraid of ten thousands of people,

That have set themselves against me round about... .
Salvation belongeth unto the Lord:
Thy blessing is upon Thy people." Psalm 3:1–8. *Patriarchs and Prophets,* 741.

There is need of prayer, earnest, fervent, agonizing prayer, such prayer as David offered when he exclaimed, "As the hart panteth after the water brooks, so panteth my soul after Thee, O God." "I have longed after Thy precepts." "I have longed for Thy salvation." "My soul longeth, yea, even fainteth for the courts of the Lord: my heart and my flesh crieth out for the living God." (Psalm 42:1; 119:40, 174; Psalm 84:2.) *Gospel Workers* (1915), 257.

David and all his company—warriors and statesmen, old men and youth, the women and the little children—in the darkness of night crossed the deep and swift-flowing river. "By the morning light there lacked not one of them that was not gone over Jordan."

David and his forces fell back to Mahanaim, which had been the royal seat of Ishbosheth. This was a strongly fortified city, surrounded by a mountainous district favorable for retreat in case of war. The country was well-provisioned, and the people were friendly to the cause of David. Here many adherents joined him, while wealthy tribesmen brought abundant gifts of provision, and other needed supplies.

Hushai's counsel had achieved its object, gaining for David opportunity for escape; but the rash and impetuous prince could not be long restrained, and he soon set out in pursuit of his father. "And Absalom passed over Jordan, he and all the men of Israel with him." Absalom made Amasa, the son of David's sister Abigail, commander-in-chief of his forces. His army was large, but it was undisciplined and poorly prepared to cope with the tried soldiers of his father.

David divided his forces into three battalions under the command of Joab, Abishai, and Ittai the Gittite. It had been his purpose himself to lead his army in the field; but against this the officers of the army, the counselors, and the people vehemently protested. "Thou shalt not go forth," they said: "for if we flee away, they will not care for us; neither if half of us die, will they care for us: but thou art worth ten thousand of us: therefore now it is better that thou be ready to succour us out of the city. And the king said unto them, What seemeth you best I will do." 2 Samuel 18:3, 4, R.V.

The Rebellion Defeated

From the walls of the city the long lines of the rebel army were in full view. The usurper was accompanied by a vast host, in comparison with which David's force seemed but a handful. But as the king looked upon the opposing forces, the thought uppermost in his mind was not of the crown and the kingdom, nor of his own life, that depended upon the wage of battle. The father's heart was filled with love and pity for his rebellious son. As the army filed out from the city gates David encouraged his faithful soldiers, bidding them go forth trusting that the God of Israel would give them the victory. But even here he could not repress his love for Absalom. As Joab, leading the first column, passed his king, the conqueror of a hundred battlefields stooped his proud head to hear the monarch's last message, as with trembling voice he said, "Deal gently for my sake with the young man, even with Absalom." And Abishai and Ittai received the same charge— "Deal gently for my sake with the young man, even with Absalom." But the king's solicitude, seeming to declare that Absalom was dearer to him than his kingdom, dearer even than the subjects faithful to his throne, only increased the indignation of the soldiers against the unnatural son.

The place of battle was a wood near the Jordan, in which the great numbers of Absalom's army were only a disadvantage to him.

Among the thickets and marshes of the forest these undisciplined troops became confused and unmanageable. And "the people of Israel were slain before the servants of David, and there was there a great slaughter that day of twenty thousand men." Absalom, seeing that the day was lost, had turned to flee, when his head was caught between the branches of a widespreading tree, and his mule going out from under him, he was left helplessly suspended, a prey to his enemies. In this condition he was found by a soldier, who, for fear of displeasing the king, spared Absalom, but reported to Joab what he had seen. Joab was restrained by no scruples. He had befriended Absalom, having twice secured his reconciliation with David, and the trust had been shamelessly betrayed. But for the advantages gained by Absalom through Joab's intercession, this rebellion, with all its horrors, could never have occurred. Now it was in Joab's power at one blow to destroy the instigator of all this evil. "And he took three darts in his hand, and thrust them through the heart of Absalom ... And they took Absalom, and cast him into a great pit in the wood, and laid a very great heap of stones upon him."

Thus perished the instigators of rebellion in Israel. Ahithophel had died by his own hand. The princely Absalom, whose glorious beauty had been the pride of Israel, had been cut down in the vigor of his youth, his dead body thrust into a pit, and covered with a heap of stones, in token of everlasting reproach. During his lifetime Absalom had reared for himself a costly monument in the king's dale, but the only memorial which marked his grave was that heap of stones in the wilderness. *Patriarchs and Prophets,* 742–744.

David Mourns for Absalom

The victorious army, returning from the field, approached the city, their shouts of triumph awaking the echoes of the hills. But as they entered the city gate the shout died away, their banners drooped in their hands, and with downcast gaze they advanced more like those who had suffered defeat than like conquerors. For the king was not waiting to bid them welcome, but from the chamber above the gate his wailing cry was heard, "O my son Absalom! my son, my son Absalom! would God I had died for thee, O Absalom, my son, my son!"

"The victory that day was turned into mourning unto all the people; for the people heard say that day how the king was grieved for his son. And the people gat them by stealth that day into the city, as people being ashamed steal away when they flee in battle."

Joab was filled with indignation. God had given them reason for triumph and gladness; the greatest rebellion that had ever been known in Israel had been crushed; and yet this great victory was turned to mourning for him whose crime had cost the blood of thousands of brave men. The rude, blunt captain pushed his way into the presence of the king, and boldly said, "Thou hast shamed this day the faces of all thy servants, which this day have saved thy life, and the lives of thy sons and of thy daughters; ... in that thou lovest thine enemies, and hatest thy friends. For thou hast declared this day, that thou regardest neither princes nor servants: for this day I perceive, that if Absalom had lived, and all we had died this day, then it had pleased thee well. Now therefore arise, go forth, and speak comfortably unto thy servants: for I swear by the Lord, if thou go not forth, there will not tarry one with thee this night: and that will be worse unto thee than all the evil that befell thee from thy youth until now."

Harsh and even cruel as was the reproof to the heart-stricken king, David did not resent it. Seeing that his general was right, he went down to the gate, and with words of courage and commendation greeted his brave soldiers as they marched past him. *Patriarchs and Prophets,* 744, 745.

Chapter Seven

The King's Final Years

The closing years of David's life were marked with faithful devotion to God. He mourned over his sins and departure from God's just precepts, which had darkened his character, and given occasion for the enemies of the Lord to blaspheme. *Spirit of Prophecy,* vol. 1, 387.

One Last Rebellion

Still another shadow was to gather over the last years of David. He had reached the age of threescore and ten. The hardships and exposures of his early wanderings, his many wars, the cares and afflictions of his later years, had sapped the fountain of life. Though his mind retained its clearness and strength, feebleness and age, with their desire for seclusion, prevented a quick apprehension of what was passing in the kingdom, and again rebellion sprang up in the very shadow of the throne. Again the fruit of David's parental indulgence was manifest. The one who now aspired to the throne was Adonijah, "a very goodly man" in person and bearing, but unprincipled and reckless. In his youth he had been subjected to but little restraint; for "his father had not displeased him at any time in saying, Why hast thou done so?" He now rebelled against the authority of God, who had appointed Solomon to the throne. Both by natural endowments and religious character Solomon was better qualified than his elder brother to become ruler of Israel; yet although the choice of God had been clearly indicated, Adonijah did not fail to find sympathizers. Joab, though guilty of many crimes, had heretofore been loyal to the throne; but he now joined the conspiracy against Solomon, as did also Abiathar the priest.

The rebellion was ripe; the conspirators had assembled at a great feast just without the city to proclaim Adonijah king, when their plans were thwarted by the prompt action of a few faithful persons, chief among whom were Zadok the priest, Nathan the prophet, and Bathsheba the mother of Solomon. They represented the state of affairs to the king, reminding him of the divine direction that Solomon should succeed to the throne. David at once abdicated in favor of Solomon, who was immediately anointed and proclaimed king. The conspiracy was crushed. Its chief actors had incurred the penalty of death. Abiathar's life was spared, out of respect to his office and his former fidelity to David; but he was degraded from the office of high priest, which passed to the line of Zadok. Joab and Adonijah were spared for the time, but after the death of David they suffered the penalty of their crime. The execution of the sentence upon the son of David completed the fourfold judgment that testified to God's abhorrence of the father's sin. *Patriarchs and Prophets,* 749.

David Plans the Temple

...The Lord, through his angel, instructed David, and gave him a pattern of the house which Solomon should build for him. An angel was commissioned to stand by David while he was writing out, for the benefit of Solomon, the important directions in regard to the arrangement of the house. David's heart was in the work. He manifested an earnestness and devotion in making extensive preparations for the building, and spared neither labor nor expense, but made large donations from his own treasury, thereby setting a noble example before his people, which they did not hesitate to follow with willing hearts. *Spirit of Prophecy,* vol. 1, 387.

From the very opening of David's reign one of his most cherished plans had been that of erecting a temple to the Lord

From the very opening of David's reign one of his most cherished plans had been that of erecting a temple to the Lord. Though he had not been permitted to execute this design, he had manifested no less zeal and earnestness in its behalf. He had provided an abundance of the most costly material—gold, silver, onyx stones, and stones of divers colors; marble, and the most precious woods. And now these valuable treasures that he had collected must be committed to others; for other hands must build the house for the ark, the symbol of God's presence. *Patriarchs and Prophets,* 750.

The true object of education should be carefully considered. God has intrusted to each one capacities and powers, that they may be returned to Him enlarged and improved. All His gifts are granted to us to be used to the utmost. He requires every one of us to cultivate our powers, and attain the highest possible capacity for usefulness, that we may do noble work for God, and bless humanity. Every talent that we possess, whether of mental capacity, money, or influence, is of God, so that we may say with David, "All things come of Thee, and of Thine own have we given Thee." *Fundamentals of Christian Education,* 82.

Seeing that his end was near, the king summoned the princes of Israel, with representative men from all parts of the kingdom, to receive this legacy in trust. He desired to commit to them his dying charge and secure their concurrence and support in the great work to be accomplished. Because of his physical weakness, it had not been expected that he would attend to this transfer in person; but the inspiration of God came upon him, and with more than his wonted fervor and power, he was able, for the last time, to address his people. He told them of his own desire to build the temple, and of the Lord's command that the work should be committed to Solomon his son. The divine assurance was, "Solomon thy son, he shall build My house and My courts; for I have chosen him to be My son, and I will be his Father. Moreover I will establish his kingdom forever, if he be constant to do My commandments and My judgments, as at this day." "Now therefore," David said, "in the sight of all Israel the congregation of the Lord, and in the audience of our God, keep and seek for all the commandments of the Lord your God: that ye may possess this good land, and leave it for an inheritance for your children after you forever." *Patriarchs and Prophets,* 750.

David feels the greatest solicitude for Solomon. He fears that he may follow his example in wrong-doing. He can see with the deepest sorrow the spots and blemishes he has brought upon his character by falling into grievous sins; and he would save his son from the evil if he could. He has learned by experience that the Lord will in no case sanction wrong-doing, whether it be found in the loftiest prince or the humblest subject, but would visit the leader of his people with as much severer punishment as his position is more responsible than that of the humblest subject. The sins committed by the leaders of Israel would have an influence to lessen the heinousness of crime in the minds and consciences of the people, and would be brought to the notice of other nations, who fear not God, but who trample upon his authority; and they would be led to blaspheme the God of Israel. *Spirit of Prophecy,* vol. 1, 387.

Parents must exercise unceasing watchfulness, that their children be not lost to God. The vows of David, recorded in the 101st Psalm, should be the vows of all upon whom rest the responsibilities of guarding the influences of the home. The psalmist declares: "I will set no wicked thing before mine eyes: I hate the work of them that turn aside; it shall not cleave to me. A froward heart shall depart from me: I will not know a wicked person. Whoso privily slandereth his neighbour, him will I cut off: him that hath an high look and a proud heart will not I suffer. Mine eyes shall be upon the faithful of the land, that they may dwell with me: he that walketh in a perfect way, he shall serve me. He that worketh deceit shall not dwell within my house: he that telleth lies shall not tarry in my sight." *Adventist Home,* 408.

> *Parents must exercise unceasing watchfulness, that their children be not lost to God*

David solemnly charges his son to adhere strictly to the law of God, and to keep all his statutes. "... And thou, Solomon, my son, know thou the God of thy father, and serve him with a perfect heart, and with a willing mind; for the Lord searcheth all hearts, and understandeth all the imaginations of the thoughts. If thou seek him, he will be found of thee; but if thou forsake him, he will cast thee off forever. Take heed now; for the Lord hath chosen thee to build an house for the sanctuary. Be strong, and do it."

After giving this charge to his son in the audience of the people, and in the presence of God, he offers grateful thanks to God for disposing his own heart, and the hearts of the people, to give willingly for the great work of building. He also entreats the Lord to incline the heart of Solomon to his commandments. He says, "I know also, my God, that thou triest the heart, and hast pleasure in uprightness. As for me, in the uprightness of mine heart I have willingly offered all these things. And now have I seen with joy thy people, which are present here to offer willingly unto thee. O Lord God of Abraham, Isaac, and of Israel, our fathers, keep this forever in the imagination of the thoughts of the heart of thy people, and prepare their heart unto thee. And give unto Solomon, my son, a perfect heart, to keep thy commandments, thy testimonies, and thy statutes, and to do all these things, and to build the palace, for the which I have made provision." *Spirit of Prophecy,* vol. 1, 388–389.

David's Final Charge

When he felt that death was approaching, the burden of David's heart was still for Solomon and for the kingdom of Israel, whose prosperity must so largely depend upon the fidelity of her king. "And he charged Solomon his son, saying, I go the way of all the earth: be thou strong therefore, and show thyself a man; and keep the charge of the Lord thy God, to walk in His ways, to keep His statutes, and His commandments, and His judgments, and His testimonies, ... that thou mayest prosper in all that thou doest, and whithersoever thou turnest thyself: that the Lord may continue His word which He spake concerning me, saying, If thy children take heed to their way, to walk before Me in truth with all their heart and with all their soul, there shall not fail thee (said He) a man on the throne of Israel." 1 Kings 2:1–4.

David's "last words," as recorded, are a song—a song of trust, of loftiest principle, and undying faith:

"David the son of Jesse saith,

And the man who was raised on high saith, The anointed of the God of Jacob,

And the sweet psalmist of Israel:

The Spirit of Jehovah spake by me: ... One that ruleth over men righteously, That ruleth in the fear of God,

He shall be as the light of the morning, when the sun riseth, A morning without clouds;

When the tender grass springeth out of the earth,

Through clear shining after rain. Verily my house is not so with God;

The King's Final Years | 113

Yet He hath made me an everlasting covenant, Ordered in all things, and sure:

For it is all my salvation, and all my desire."
2 Samuel 23:1–5, R.V.

Great had been David's fall, but deep was his repentance, ardent was his love, and strong his faith. He had been forgiven much, and therefore he loved much. Luke 7:47.

The psalms of David pass through the whole range of experience, from the depths of conscious guilt and self-condemnation to the loftiest faith and the most exalted communing with God. His life record declares that sin can bring only shame and woe, but that God's love and mercy can reach to the deepest depths, that faith will lift up the repenting soul to share the adoption of the sons of God. Of all the assurances which His word contains, it is one of the strongest testimonies to the faithfulness, the justice, and the covenant mercy of God. *Patriarchs and Prophets,* 753, 754.

Bibliography

Books

Adventist Home. Hagerstown, MD: Review and Herald Publishing Association, 1952.

Conflict and Courage. Washington, DC: Review and Herald Publishing Association, 1970.

Education. Mountain View, CA: Pacific Press Publishing Association, 1903.

Fundamentals of Christian Education. Nashville, TN: Southern Publishing Association, 1923.

Gospel Workers Battle Creek, MI: Review and Herald Publishing Association, 1892.

Gospel Workers Washington, DC: Review and Herald Publishing Association, 1915.

Ministry of Healing, The. Mountain View, CA: Pacific Press Publishing Association, 1905.

Patriarchs and Prophets. Washington, DC: Review and Herald Publishing Association, 1890.

SDA Bible Commentary, The, Vol. 2. Washington, DC: Review and Herald Publishing Association, 1953.

SDA Bible Commentary, The, Vol. 3. Washington, DC: Review and Herald Publishing Association, 1954.

Spirit of Prophecy, Vol. 1. Battle Creek, MI: Seventh-day Adventist Publishing Association, 1870.

Spiritual Gifts, Vol. 4a. Battle Creek, MI: Seventh-day Adventist Publishing Association, 1864.

Spiritual Gifts, Vol. 4. Battle Creek, MI: Seventh-day Adventist Publishing Association, 1864.

Testimonies for the Church, Vol. 5. Mountain View, CA: Pacific Press Publishing Association, 1889.

Periodicals

Our Australian Youth, 3/1/1888.

Review and Herald, Jan. 22, 1880.

Signs of the Times, 3/4/1886 thru 8/8/1895.

Manuscripts

Manuscript Releases, Vol. 21. Silver Spring, MD: Ellen G. White Estate, 1993.

Original sources were used except when a condensed version from a later source was fitting.

TEACH Services, Inc.
P U B L I S H I N G

We invite you to view the complete
selection of titles we publish at:
www.TEACHServices.com

We encourage you to write us
with your thoughts about this,
or any other book we publish at:
info@TEACHServices.com

TEACH Services' titles may be purchased in
bulk quantities for educational, fund-raising,
business, or promotional use.
bulksales@TEACHServices.com

Finally, if you are interested in seeing
your own book in print, please contact us at:
publishing@TEACHServices.com
We are happy to review your manuscript at no charge.

www.ingramcontent.com/pod-product-compliance
Lightning Source LLC
Chambersburg PA
CBHW070557160426
43199CB00014B/2533